First World War
and Army of Occupation
War Diary
France, Belgium and Germany

14 DIVISION
Divisional Troops
King's (Liverpool Regiment)
11th Battalion Pioneers
17 May 1915 - 31 May 1918

WO95/1890/5

The Naval & Military Press Ltd
www.nmarchive.com
Published in association with The National Archives

Published by

The Naval & Military Press Ltd

Unit 10 Ridgewood Industrial Park,

Uckfield, East Sussex,

TN22 5QE England

Tel: +44 (0) 1825 749494

www.naval-military-press.com

www.nmarchive.com

This diary has been reprinted in facsimile from the original. Any imperfections are inevitably reproduced and the quality may fall short of modern type and cartographic standards.

© **Crown Copyright**
Images reproduced by permission of The National Archives, London, England, 2015.

Contents

Document type	Place/Title	Date From	Date To
Heading	WO95/1890/5		
Heading	14th Division 11th Bn King's L'Pool Regt (Pioneer Bn) May 1915-May 1918. Returned To UK 1918 June		
Heading	14th Division 11th Liverpool Regt Vol I 17-31.5.15 May 15 To May 18		
Heading	War Diary Of 11th Battn The King's (Liverpool) Regt (Pioneers) From 17.5.15 To 31.5.15		
War Diary	Watts Common Aldershot	17/05/1915	18/05/1915
War Diary	Rubrouck	19/05/1915	26/05/1915
War Diary	Vlamertinghe	26/05/1915	31/05/1915
Heading	14th Division 11th Liverpools (Pioneer) Vol II 1-30.6.15		
War Diary	Vlamertinghe	01/06/1915	11/06/1915
War Diary	Ypres	11/06/1915	14/06/1915
War Diary	Vlamertinghe	15/06/1915	20/06/1915
War Diary	Ypres	21/06/1915	30/06/1915
Heading	14th Division 11th Liverpools (Pioneers) Vol III 1-31.7.15		
Heading	War Diary Of 11th Battn The King's (Liverpool) Regt (Pioneers) From July 1st 1915 To July 31st 1915 (Volume 3)		
War Diary	Ypres	01/07/1915	31/07/1915
Heading	14th Division 11th Kings Liverpools Rgt (Pioneers) Vol 4 Aug To Oct 15		
Heading	War Diary Of 11th Bn King's (Liverpool) Regiment (Pioneers) From 1st August To 31st October		
War Diary	Ypres	01/08/1915	23/10/1915
War Diary	Watou	24/10/1915	31/10/1915
Miscellaneous	Copy Of Messages From Major General Coupee	10/10/1915	10/10/1915
Heading	14th Division 11th Liverpools Vol 5 Nov 15		
Heading	War Diary Of 11th Bn King's Liverpool Regiment (Pioneers) From 1st November To 30th November 1915 Volume 6		
War Diary	Watou	01/11/1915	19/11/1915
War Diary	Ypres	20/11/1915	30/11/1915
Heading	14th 11th L'pools Vol 6 Dec		
Heading	War Diary Of 11th Bn Kings Liverpool Regt (Pioneers) From 1st December 1915 To 31st December 1915 (Volume 7)		
War Diary	Ypres	01/12/1915	15/12/1915
War Diary	Watou	15/12/1915	31/12/1915
War Diary	Elverdinghe	01/01/1916	01/01/1916
Miscellaneous	14th Division	21/12/1915	21/12/1915
Miscellaneous	14th Division Return In Accordance With 14th Division Routine Order No. 1029 Dated 18.12.15	20/12/1915	20/12/1915
Miscellaneous	Roll Of Officers 11th (S) Bn. The King's Liverpool Regt. (Pioneers)		
Heading	14 Pioneers 11th L'pools Vol 7		

Heading	War Diary Of 11th (S) Bn. The King's Liverpool Regt. (Pioneers) From 1st January 1916 To 31st January 1916 (Volume VIII)		
War Diary	Elverdinghe	01/01/1916	01/02/1916
Heading	11th Kings Liverpools Vol 8 14th Div		
Heading	War Diary Of 11th (S) Bn. The King's Liverpool Regt. (Pioneers) From 1st February 1916 To 29th February 1916 (Volume VIII)		
War Diary	Elverdinghe	01/02/1916	10/02/1916
War Diary	A 16 a Sheet 28 No 1 Camp	11/02/1916	12/02/1916
War Diary	Ledringhem	19/02/1916	19/02/1916
War Diary	Cassel Longueau	20/02/1916	20/02/1916
War Diary	Ledringhem	19/02/1916	19/02/1916
War Diary	Cassel Longueau	20/02/1916	20/02/1916
War Diary	Villers Bocage	20/02/1916	24/02/1916
War Diary	Authieule	25/02/1916	25/02/1916
War Diary	Warlurzel	26/02/1916	28/02/1916
War Diary	Fosseux	28/02/1916	04/03/1916
War Diary	Dainville	05/03/1916	11/03/1916
War Diary	Arras	12/03/1916	31/03/1916
Heading	War Diary Of 11th (S) Bn Kings Liverpool Regiment (Pioneers) From 1st April 1916 To 30th April 1916 (Volume X)		
War Diary	Arras	01/04/1916	31/05/1916
Heading	War Diary Of 11th (S) Bn. The King's Liverpool Regt. (Pioneers) From 1st June 1916 To 30th June 1916 (Volume XII)		
War Diary	Arras	01/06/1916	30/06/1916
War Diary	War Diary Of 11 Liverpool Regiment (Pioneers) From July 1st To July 31st 1916 (Volume 13)		
Miscellaneous	14th Division	31/07/1916	31/07/1916
Heading	War Diary Of 11th (S) Bn. The King's Liverpool Regt. (Pioneers) From 1st July 1916 To 31st July 1916 (Volume XIII)		
War Diary	Arras	01/07/1916	27/07/1916
War Diary	Ivergny	28/07/1916	29/07/1916
War Diary	Outrebois Frohen Le Grand	30/07/1916	31/07/1916
Heading	War Diary Of 11th (S) Bn. The King's Liverpool Regt. (Pioneers) From 1st August 1916 To 31st August 1916 (Volume XIV)		
War Diary	Beaumetz	01/08/1916	07/08/1916
War Diary	1000 Sdes S.W. Albert E.9.a.7.8 France 1/40,000 Sheet 62d	08/08/1916	12/08/1916
War Diary	F.9.a Sheet 62d	13/08/1916	18/08/1916
War Diary	F.9.a Sheet 62D France 1:40,000	18/08/1916	30/08/1916
Heading	War Diary Of 11th Bn. "The King's" Liverpool Regt (Pioneers) From 1st September 1916 To 30th September 1916 (Volume XV)		
War Diary	Tailly Ref Map Dieppe 16	01/09/1916	11/09/1916
War Diary	Dernacourt	12/09/1916	12/09/1916
War Diary	Fricourt Wood	13/09/1916	14/09/1916
War Diary	S.23.c. Sheet 57c 1:40,000	15/09/1916	16/09/1916
War Diary	Fricourt Wood	17/09/1916	17/09/1916
War Diary	D18.b. Sheet 62D	18/09/1916	22/09/1916
War Diary	Ivergny	23/09/1916	26/09/1916
War Diary	Berneville	26/09/1916	30/09/1916

Heading	War Diary Of 11th. Bn. The King's (Liverpool) Regt. (Pioneers) From 1st October 1916 To 31st October 1916 (Volume XVI)		
War Diary	Berneville	01/10/1916	31/10/1916
Heading	War Diary Of 11th Bn The King's (Liverpool) Regt (Pioneers) From 1st November 1916 To 30th November 1916 (Volume XVII)		
War Diary	Berneville	01/11/1916	05/11/1916
War Diary	Gouy-En-Artois	06/11/1916	08/11/1916
War Diary	Buneville	09/11/1916	30/11/1916
Heading	War Diary Of 11th Bn The King's Liverpool Regt (Pioneers) From 1st December 1916 To 31st December 1916 (Volume XVIII)		
War Diary	Buneville	01/12/1916	17/12/1916
War Diary	Dinier	18/12/1916	18/12/1916
War Diary	Buneville	19/12/1916	31/12/1916
Heading	War Diary Of 11th Bn The King's (Liverpool) Regt (Pioneers) From 1st January 1917 To 31st January 1917 (Volume XIX)		
Miscellaneous	14th Division	01/02/1917	01/02/1917
War Diary	Berneville	01/01/1917	31/01/1917
Heading	War Diary Of 11th (S) Bn. "The King's" (Liverpool) Regiment (Pioneers) From 1st February 1917 To 28th February 1917 (Volume XX)		
Miscellaneous	14th Division	01/03/1917	01/03/1917
War Diary	Dainville	01/02/1917	04/02/1917
War Diary	Arras	05/02/1917	28/02/1917
Heading	War Diary Of 11th Bn. "The King's" (Liverpool) Regt (Pioneers) From 1st March 1917 To 31st March 1917 (Volume XXI)		
War Diary	Arras	01/03/1917	31/03/1917
Heading	War Diary Of 11th (S) Bn. The King's Liverpool Regt. (Pioneers) From 1st April 1917 To 30th April 1917 (Volume) XXII		
War Diary	Arras	01/04/1917	11/04/1917
War Diary	Dainville	12/04/1917	12/04/1917
War Diary	Habarcq	13/04/1917	13/04/1917
War Diary	Grand Rullecourt	14/04/1917	23/04/1917
War Diary	Pommier	24/04/1917	24/04/1917
War Diary	Bailleulmont	25/04/1917	27/04/1917
War Diary	Arras	28/04/1917	29/04/1917
War Diary	Telegraph Hill	30/04/1917	30/04/1917
Heading	War Diary Of 11th Bn The King's (Liverpool) Regt (Pioneers) From 1st May 1917 To 31st May 1917 (Volume XXIII)		
War Diary	Telegraph Hill	01/05/1917	31/05/1917
Heading	War Diary Of 11th (S) Bn. The King's (Liverpool) Regt (Pioneers) From 1st June 1917 To 30th June 1917 (Volume XXIV)		
Miscellaneous	14th Division	01/07/1917	01/07/1917
War Diary	Telegraph Hill	01/06/1917	06/06/1917
War Diary	Neuville Vitasse	07/06/1917	13/06/1917
War Diary	St. Leger-Le-Authie	14/06/1917	28/06/1917
War Diary	Locre	29/06/1917	30/06/1917

Heading	War Diary Of 11th Bn. The King's (Liverpool) Regt (Pioneers) From 1st July 1917 To 31st July 1917 (Volume XXV)		
War Diary	Kemmel	01/07/1917	31/07/1917
Heading	War Diary Of 11th (S) Bn. The King's Liverpool Regt (Pioneers) From 1st August 1917 To 31st August 1917 (Volume XXVI)		
Miscellaneous	14th (Light) Division	01/09/1917	01/09/1917
War Diary	Kemmel	01/08/1917	05/08/1917
War Diary	N.E. Of Hazebrouck	06/08/1917	07/08/1917
War Diary	Dickebusch	08/08/1917	17/08/1917
War Diary	28 H. 33. b	18/08/1917	27/08/1917
War Diary	Near Abeele Thieushouk	28/08/1917	31/08/1917
Heading	War Diary Of 11th Bn. The King's (Liverpool) Regt. (Pioneers) From 1st September 1917 To 30th September 1917 (Volume XXVII)		
War Diary	Thieushouk Neuve Eglise	01/09/1917	03/09/1917
War Diary	Wulverghem	04/09/1917	30/09/1917
Heading	War Diary Of 11th. Bn. The King's (Liverpool) Regt (Pioneers) From 1st October 1917 To 31st October 1917 Volume XXVIII		
War Diary	Wulverghem	01/10/1917	06/10/1917
War Diary	M.17.c.3.9 Near Locre	07/10/1917	07/10/1917
War Diary	I.19.d.3.0 Dickebusch Area	08/10/1917	13/10/1917
War Diary	28/I.19.d.3.0 Dickebusch Area	14/10/1917	31/10/1917
Heading	War Diary Of 11th (S) Battn King's (L'pool) Regt (Pioneers) From 1st November 1917 To 30th November 1917 (Volume XXIX)		
Miscellaneous	14th Divn	01/12/1917	01/12/1917
War Diary	28/I.19.d.3.0 Dickebusch Area	01/11/1917	06/11/1917
War Diary	Thieushouk 27/Q.35.b.2.3	07/11/1917	09/11/1917
War Diary	Vlamertinghe Area 28.H.16.a	10/11/1917	11/11/1917
War Diary	Potijze Area 28.I.3.d	12/11/1917	28/11/1917
War Diary	St Jean Area 28/ C.27.d.9.5	29/11/1917	30/11/1917
Heading	War Diary Of 11th Battalion King's L'Pool Regt. (Pioneers) From December 1st 1917 To December 31st 1917 (Vol XXX)		
War Diary	Potijze St Jean Area 28.C.27.d.9.5	01/12/1917	07/12/1917
War Diary	La Brique 28/C.26.d.5.0	08/12/1917	31/12/1917
Heading	War Diary Of 11th (S) Battalion King's (L'Pool) Regt (Pioneers) From January 1st 1918 To January 31st 1918 (Vol XXXI)		
War Diary	St Martin Au Laert	01/01/1918	04/01/1918
War Diary	Bray Marley Camp 62D/R4.d.3.6	05/01/1918	07/01/1918
War Diary	Marley Camp 62D/R4.d.3.6	08/01/1918	15/01/1918
War Diary	Marley Camp France 62.d. R.4.d.3.6	16/01/1918	21/01/1918
War Diary	Ref Maps Amiens	22/01/1918	24/01/1918
War Diary	St Quentin	25/01/1918	28/01/1918
War Diary	Montescourt	29/01/1918	31/01/1918
Heading	War Diary 11th Bn King's (L'Pool) Regiment (Pioneers) From Feb 1st 1918 To Feb 28th 1918 (Volume XXXII)		
Miscellaneous	14th (Light) Divn	07/03/1918	07/03/1918
War Diary	Montescourt	01/02/1918	28/02/1918
Heading	War Diary 11th Bn King's Liverpool Regt (Pioneers) From March 1st 1918 To March 31st 1918 (Volume XXXIII)		

War Diary	Clastres 66C	01/03/1918	21/03/1918
War Diary	Clastres	21/03/1918	21/03/1918
War Diary	Detroit Bleu	22/03/1918	22/03/1918
War Diary	Beaumont En Beine	23/03/1918	23/03/1918
War Diary	Noyon	24/03/1918	24/03/1918
War Diary	Sermaize	25/03/1918	25/03/1918
War Diary	Thiescourt	26/03/1918	26/03/1918
War Diary	Elincourt	27/03/1918	27/03/1918
War Diary	Remy	28/03/1918	28/03/1918
War Diary	Pont Sur Maxence	29/03/1918	29/03/1918
War Diary	Creil	30/03/1918	30/03/1918
War Diary	Airion	31/03/1918	31/03/1918
Heading	War Diary 11th Battn. The King's (Liverpool Regiment). April (1/27.4.18) 1918		
Miscellaneous	14th Divn	30/04/1918	30/04/1918
War Diary	Wavignies	01/04/1918	01/04/1918
War Diary	Bonneuil	02/04/1918	02/04/1918
War Diary	Boves	03/04/1918	03/04/1918
War Diary	Aubigny	04/04/1918	06/04/1918
War Diary	Blangy Tronville	07/04/1918	07/04/1918
War Diary	St Acheul	08/04/1918	10/04/1918
War Diary	Aigneville	11/04/1918	12/04/1918
War Diary	Ergny	13/04/1918	13/04/1918
War Diary	Beaumetz Lez Aire	14/04/1918	14/04/1918
War Diary	Molinghem	15/04/1918	27/04/1918
Heading	War Diary Of 11th Bn The King's Battn Training Staff From April 27th 1918 To May 31 1918 (Volume I)		
War Diary	Molinghem Lisbourg Sains Lez Fressin	27/04/1918	01/05/1918
War Diary	Clenleu	02/05/1918	21/05/1918
War Diary	Torcy	22/05/1918	31/05/1918
Heading	11 Liverpools Vol 9		

W95/1840(S)

W95/1840(S)

14TH DIVISION

11TH BN KING'S L'POOL REGT
(PIONEER BN)
MAY 1915 - MAY 1918.

RETURNED TO UK 1918 JUNE

1.Y.
(5 sheets)

121/5482

Pioneers
14th Division.

11th Liverpool Regt.
Vol I 17 — 31. 5.15

May -15
to
May '15

CONFIDENTIAL

WAR DIARY

of

11th Battn. the King's (Liverpool) Regt (Pioneers)

from 17.5.15 to 31.5.15.

Army Form C. 2118.

WAR DIARY
or
INTELLIGENCE SUMMARY.
(Erase heading not required.)

Instructions regarding War Diaries and Intelligence Summaries are contained in F.S. Regs., Part II. and the Staff Manual respectively. Title pages will be prepared in manuscript.

Place	Date	Hour	Summary of Events and Information	Remarks and references to Appendices
WATTS COMMON ALDERSHOT.	17.5.15	10.30pm	Instructions were received that 18th May was to be the first day of Entrainment. The Transport of the Batt? to move to HAVRE via SOUTHAMPTON, the remainder of the Regt to BOULOGNE via FOLKESTONE on 19.5.15 proceeding by ½ Batt ns.	C.C.O
	1st DAY MOB N 18.5.15	7.45am 8.30am	Transport left for SOUTHAMPTON, entraining at FARNBOROUGH, L.&S.W.Ry Station.	C.C.O
RUBROUCK	2nd DAY 19.5.15 20.5.15	8.45pm 7.30pm	The Regt left WATT'S Common by ½ Batt ns to entrain at Govt SIDING, ALDERSHOT. The ½ Batt ns arrived at FOLKESTONE at 12mn and 12.30am 20.5.15, and embarked on H.M. PRINCESS VICTORIA which left FOLKESTONE at 1am arriving at BOULOGNE at 2.45am. On disembarking the Batt ns Armoury and marched to OSTROHOVE Rest Camp, which it reached at 4.10am. The Regt left Camp at 10.30am and marched to PONT-DE-BRIQUES Ry Station, where the Regimental Transport met the Battalion by train. The Regt entrained at 12noon and moved to SAVINHOVE STATION where it detrained at 5.50pm, and proceeded by march route to RUBROUCK where it went into billets at 8.20pm.	C.C.O
Do	22.5.15	11am	The Regt was inspected in its billets. Major General COUPER was present during part of the time.	C.C.O
Do	23.5.15	7am 11am	Church Parade was held at 7am for the Roman Catholics in the village Church and at 11am in a field for the C.of.E. the Officer Commanding conducting the service of the latter	C.C.O
Do	24.5.15	9.30am	The Regiment was exercised in a route march and inspected by Brigadier General MARKHAM at ERLESBRUGGE.	C.C.O
Do	25.5.15	12.40pm	Orders were received for the Regt to proceed to VLAMERTINGHE and to be attached to the 2nd Army	C.C.O
Do	26.5.15	6am 11am	The Regt left RUBROUCK for VLAMERTINGHE in 45 motor buses. On arrival the men detrained and at 9.15am marched to the wood in the Chateau grounds Square H3A where they bivouacked at 11am. They paraded and marched to the road crossing the CANAL D'YPRES, Square I19D, for the purpose of strengthening existing defence works and making communication and support trenches. They came under shell fire and suffered 4 casualties from shrapnel, all slightly wounded. The Regt returned to bivouac at 7.15 pm.	C.C.O Map Belgium Map (8 series) Sheet 28 N.W.
VLAMERTINGHE	27.5.15	7am 7.30pm	It having been thought inadvisable to expose the men to shell fire during the day A+B Coys paraded and marched to the last support portion of the trenches at 7.30 pm to continue the work Very night C+D Coys Parades commenced	C.C.O

1577 Wt.W10791/1773 500,000 1/15 D.D.&L. A.D.S.S./Forms/C. 2118.

Army Form C. 2118.

WAR DIARY
or
INTELLIGENCE SUMMARY.
(Erase heading not required.)

Instructions regarding War Diaries and Intelligence Summaries are contained in F. S. Regs., Part II. and the Staff Manual respectively. Title pages will be prepared in manuscript.

Place	Date	Hour	Summary of Events and Information	Remarks and references to Appendices
LAMERTINGHE	28.5.15	7 a.m.	A & B Coys paraded at 7 a.m. to continue the work on the defences. At 1 p.m. Shells fell in the trenches where the men were working, killing 1 and wounding 5. 2 further men seriously wounded, in	E.C.O
Do	29.5.15	7 a.m. 7 p.m.	The Regiment continued work on the defences. There was no shelling during the day or night.	E.C.O
Do	30.5.15	7 a.m. 7 p.m.	The day passed off quietly, with no shelling of or casualties. The Reg.t continued its work on the defences.	
Do	31.5.15		The Reg.t continued the work of the previous days. There were no casualties.	

2.Y.
(5 sheets)

21/5935

14th Division

11th The Liverpools (Pioneer)

Vol: II 1 — 30.6.15.

WAR DIARY or INTELLIGENCE SUMMARY

Army Form C. 2118.

11th Liverpools

(Erase heading not required.)

Instructions regarding War Diaries and Intelligence Summaries are contained in F.S. Regs., Part II. and the Staff Manual respectively. Title pages will be prepared in manuscript.

Place	Date	Hour	Summary of Events and Information	Remarks and references to Appendices
VLAMERTINGHE	1.6.15	7am / 7pm	The Reg.t paraded by ½ Batt.ns at 7am and 7pm to continue the work on the defences. There were no casualties	E.C.O
Do.	2.6.15	7am / 7pm	The work on the Trenches was continued. There was considerable shelling but the Batt.n was not affected at its work	E.C.O
Do.	3.6.15	7am / 7pm	The Batt.n continued the work on the support and communication trenches. The day passed off quietly	E.C.O
Do.	4.6.15	7am / 7pm	The work on the various trenches was continued. There was no shelling of the working parties by day or night	E.C.O
Do.	5.6.15	7am / 7pm	The various tasks were continued. The day passed off quietly	E.C.O
Do.	6.6.15	7am / 7pm	The work was continued on the trenches. There was no shelling of working parties	E.C.O
Do.	7.6.15	7am / 7pm	The Reg.t continued the work already commenced. There was some shelling but it did not interfere with the working parties. There were no casualties	E.C.O
Do.	8.6.15	7am / 7pm	The work was continued. The day passed off quietly	E.C.O
Do.	9.6.15	7am / 7pm	The companies continued work on their various tasks.	E.C.O
Do.	10.6.15	7pm	Two Companies were moved to work on communication trenches E. of YPRES. Heavy rain interfered with the work. The Corps returned to billets at 2.30 am.	E.C.O Ref.e Map Sheet 28.B Moorse Square I.15B and I.16A
Do.	11.6.15	11.15am	The Batt.n received orders to proceed to billets at YPRES. It left its bivouac at 3pm and reached its new destination at 4.30pm and was billeted as follows B+D Coy in the Infantry Barracks. A Coy in the prison C Coy in the magazine	E.C.O Ref.e Map Sheet 28.B Moorse Square I.14.D
YPRES		8.30pm	At 8.30pm the Batt.n paraded and proceeded through the LILLE gate to dig assembly trenches at Map White Post F 4". 1 suffered one casualty, wounded	E.C.O
Do.	12.6.15	8.30pm	The Batt.n paraded as on the previous day to continue work on the trenches already begun. It was shelled on the way to the work and had two casualties, wounded.	E.C.O
Do.	13.6.15	8.30pm	Work at the trenches was continued. A French mortar threw a bomb into our trenches, as a result of the explosion of which there were seven casualties, all wounded.	E.C.O

WAR DIARY or INTELLIGENCE SUMMARY

Army Form C. 2118.

(Erase heading not required.)

Instructions regarding War Diaries and Intelligence Summaries are contained in F. S. Regs., Part II. and the Staff Manual respectively. Title pages will be prepared in manuscript.

Place	Date	Hour	Summary of Events and Information	Remarks and references to Appendices
YPRES	14.6.15	1.45 p.m.	Orders were received for the Batt.n to return to its former billets at VLAMERTINGHE at the conclusion of the night's work.	
		8.30 p.m.	The Batt.n marched out to continue work in the Trenches. There was considerable amount of shelling both while it was going to the Trenches and while there, as a result of which the work was considerably delayed. There are three casualties, all wounded. It returned to billets at VLAMERTINGHE at 3.30 a.m. 15.6.15.	C.C.O
VLAMERTINGHE	15.6.15		The Batt.n remained in billets. A draft of 119 other ranks arrived from England.	C.C.O
Do.	16.5.15		The Batt.n remained in its billets	C.C.O
Do.	17.6.15		The Batt.n remained in billets	C.C.O
Do.	18.6.15		The Batt.n remained in billets	C.C.O
Do.	19.6.15	5.30 p.m.	Orders were received for the Batt.n to proceed to YPRES on 20.6 to take over billets from the Middlesex Reg.t who were in dug outs on the ramparts in Square I 8 D 1.6.	C.C.O Reg.tal Sheet map 2.B.D. 1/40,000 C.C.O
Do.	20.6.15	7 p.m.	Acting under the orders received on 19.6. the Batt.n marched off by companies, starting at 7 p.m. and it had been found that the dug-outs were not sufficient to give accommodation to the whole Batt.n the Reg.t occupied its old billets in YPRES, namely A Coy the PRISON, C Coy the magazine, B and D Coy the Infantry Barracks. Instructions were received to place one Coy at the disposal of the 42nd Inf.y Bde to form a Bde workshop and to assist the R.E. generally.	C.C.O
YPRES	21.6.15		As a result of the instructions received the previous evening the first Bde workshop was formed under Lieut. GOODACRE and 20 men, from the 42nd Inf.y Bde. in some sheds near the Pallyport Do door on the Canal. It has obtained work on "repairs on trench boards, knife rests, rifle rests, getting set.s for lining the Trenches, and on sawing canvas for tents, and for signboards to be painted.	
		8.30 p.m.	A Coy and 2 platoons C Coy paraded for trench work and proceeded to Square I 10 B and Square I 10 D. Two casualties both wounded, one severely, were reported.	Ref.l Map 28 13 1/10,000 C.C.O
Do.	22.6.15		The idea of Bde workshops was extended and one was formed for the 45th Inf.y Bde under Cap.t TROTTER and 25 men. The same trench materials were required as before and also pavements, crosses. Considerable difficulty was experienced in getting material in sufficient quantities for this as the orders against removing material from houses were strict.	
		8.30 p.m.	Work on the Trenches was continued. 1/2 Coy working in Square I 5 T 3 and I 16 A on a communication trench, and 1/2 Coy was to dig communication trenches in Square I 11 388 and I 24 08. Casualties 1 killed. Two wounded, 1 accidentally wounded. A. C. and D Coys were employed on this.	C.C.O

WAR DIARY or INTELLIGENCE SUMMARY.

Army Form C. 2118.

Instructions regarding War Diaries and Intelligence Summaries are contained in F.S. Regs., Part II. and the Staff Manual respectively. Title pages will be prepared in manuscript.

(Erase heading not required.)

Place	Date	Hour	Summary of Events and Information	Remarks and references to Appendices
YPRES	23.6.15	9 a.m.	Lieut Col. BAILEY with CAPT BROWNE, CAPT TROTTER and LIEUT GOODACRE went to ARMENTIERES to see the workshops of the 2nd Army and to get ideas regarding the workdone there and returned at 5.30 p.m.	E.C.O
Do	24.6.15	8.30 p.m.	The Batt. continued work on the trenches. The night proved up quietly. There were now three B.C. workshops. Lieut STANTON having formed one for the art. Sh.A. Bty. Co. a month of the visit to ARMENTIERES it was decided to send 30 N.C.O's and men, belonging to the following trades Carpenters, Wheelwrights, Tin smiths and fitters to ARMENTIERES to undergo a course of instruction in the 2nd Army workshops. Permission was asked for and given and the men were under Sergt WILLIS. B Coy sent wounded to proceed the following morning.	E.C.O
Do	25.6.15	9 a.m.	Work was continued in the trenches and there were no casualties during the working parties, but during the afternoon a shell burst over the Infantry Barracks and three men were wounded.	E.C.O
		8.30 p.m.	The 30 N.C.O's and men marched to VIAMERTINGHE where two trams were waiting to convey them to ARMENTIERES. By this time the workshops were able to cope with most of the requirements of the various Brigades. Though the work of one or two missions was felt.	
Do	26.6.15	7.30 a.m.	Further work on the trenches was carried out, though hindered by rain. A draft of 40 other ranks arrived from ENGLAND	E.C.O
			A party of 50 men under 2/Lieut GRAY was asked for and detailed to assist the 10th Division Signal Officer in laying a cable and wires to Ypres Barracks.	
Do	27.6.15	8.30 p.m.	Work on the trenches was continued. There was some shelling during the night and one casualty wounded.	E.C.O
Do	28.6.15	8.30 p.m.	There was no casualties among the working parties but this man was wounded while asleep	E.C.O
Do	29.6.15	8.30 p.m.	Work was continued. There was one casualty wounded. Major J. YPRES. Through him and Lieut ZONDAK, the Belgian representative, town Major of YPRES	E.C.O
			Lieut Col. WICKHAM was appointed Belgian representative furnishing us received to procure from known such was required in the workshops, for the purchasing of French equipments. These workshops were better able to offer such orders as they received, a list which we sent to the Belgian representative each day.	E.C.O
Do	30.6.15	8.30 p.m.	The trenches were further improved. There was one casualty wounded	E.C.O

1577 Wt.W10791/1773 500,000 1/15 D. D. & L. A.D.S.S./Forms/C. 2118.

121/6357

3.Y.
(7 sheets)

14th Division

11th Liverpools (Pioneers)

Vol: III

Nov 1-31. Jan 15

CONFIDENTIAL

WAR DIARY

of

11th Battⁿ the King's (Liverpool) Reg^t (Pioneers)

from July 1st 1915   to July 31st 1915

(Volume 3)

Army Form C. 2118.

WAR DIARY
or
INTELLIGENCE SUMMARY.
(Erase heading not required.)

Place	Date	Hour	Summary of Events and Information	Remarks and references to Appendices
YPRES	1.7.15	8.30pm	There was one casualty among the working parties on this night, wounded.	8 C.O
Do	2.7.15		It was decided that the C.R.E. should have general supervision over all the 13th workshops, so as to regulate the manufacture and issue of all stores required in the trenches. A request for two officers huts to be built in N.10.c. for the Headquarters 43rd Infy Bde was received. The making and erecting of the huts was carried out by Capt TROTTER. A draft of 28 other ranks arrived from England. One man was wounded by the bursting of a shell near the 43rd Bde Workshops.	Reft Sheet 28 B 1/40000 8 C.O 6 C.O 6 C.O
Do	3.7.15			
Do	4.7.15		Orders were received to attach the two machine guns belonging to the Battalion to the 41st Infy Bde on the night 5/6 July	
Do	5.7.15		Acting under the orders received the previous evening the two machine gun section under Lieut. PAGET and Sgt RICHARDS paraded at 7.30 pm and marched off to relieve the machine gun section of the 6th D.C.L.I. in the trenches. During the effect of a shell the forge of one of the Battn workshops was wrecked but fortunately no one was injured.	
		8.30pm	The Battalion suffered the following casualties that evening while digging trenches. 1 killed 3 wounded, all belonging to "C" Coy.	6 C.O
Do	6.7.15	8.30pm	There were no working parties on this day, the men having been given a days rest	6 C.O
Do	7.7.15	8.30pm	The Battn. continued work on the trenches	6 C.O
Do	8.7.15	8.30pm	One man was wounded during the night while working at the trenches. The 18th Machine Gun Officer recommended that the Battn machine gun section should be relieved from the trenches on the night 10/11 July, as the 41st Infy Bde were being relieved by the 42nd Infy Bde	6 C.O

Army Form C. 2118.

Instructions regarding War Diaries and Intelligence Summaries are contained in F.S. Regs., Part II. and the Staff Manual respectively. Title pages will be prepared in manuscript.

WAR DIARY
or
INTELLIGENCE SUMMARY.
(Erase heading not required.)

Place	Date	Hour	Summary of Events and Information	Remarks and references to Appendices
YPRES.	9.7.15	3.30pm	A draft of 20 other ranks arrived from ENGLAND	E.C.O
Do	10.7.15		The transport personnel moved their billets from A.28.c. to H.7.a.0.8. on instructions from H.Q. The existing communication trenches were further widened and built up. There were no casualties.	E.C.O R/s Map 28.B. 1:40,000
Do.	11.7.15	8.30p-	The machine gun section in the trenches under 2/Lieut. PAGET was relieved by the Reserve Section under 2/Lieut. BRERETON and Sergt. RAWSON on this date, having been in the trenches for seven days.	E.C.O
Do	12.7.15	8.30pm	During the night work on the trenches one man was severely wounded.	E.C.O
Do	13.7.15	8.30p	Two men were wounded during trench digging.	E.C.O
Do	14.7.15	8.30pm	One of the machine guns was put out of action by a shell, and two men wounded during the night shift, and one man was wounded while digging in the trenches. The 14th Division asked for the services of 10 signallers from the Batt. to assist the 14th Signal Coy in maintaining communications. Major BESANT took over the duties of Town Major from Lieut. Col. WICKHAM. 2/Lt LEADBETTER was relieved to report to the O/off the Depot HELFAUT for duty in connection with Gas. Sergt. THOMPSON relieved Sgt RAWSON with the machine guns at the trenches. The latter having been sent to hospital sick.	E.C.O
Do	16.7.15	6.30p	The work on the trenches was much hindered by heavy rain. Sgt THOMPSON of the machine gun section was wounded. Orders were received for the section to be relieved by the section of the 43rd Sept 13th on the night 18/19 July.	E.C.O
Do	17.7.15		One man was wounded in the trenches this evening.	E.C.O
Do	18.7.15		The machine Gun section was relieved this night and returned to billets at 11.15pm. Lieut. PATON was sent to hospital sick. The Batt has the hot baths at POPERINGHE placed at its disposal. Five men were wounded during the day at work at French work.	E.C.O
Do	19.7.15			
Do	20.7.15		Five men were wounded during the morning at trench work. The night working parties were cancelled on account of the heavy firing in front	E.C.O

1577 Wt.W10791/1773 500,000 1/15 D.D. & L. A.D.S.S./Forms/C. 2118.

Army Form C. 2118.

WAR DIARY
or
INTELLIGENCE SUMMARY.
(Erase heading not required.)

Instructions regarding War Diaries and Intelligence Summaries are contained in F. S. Regs., Part II. and the Staff Manual respectively. Title pages will be prepared in manuscript.

Place	Date	Hour	Summary of Events and Information	Remarks and references to Appendices
YPRES	20/7/15	6.30p.m.	(Cont'd) The disposal of the working parties was now left to M.C.O., and there were detailed by him instead of by the R.E. as heretofore. In consequence two companies do work at night and the remaining two continue that work by day so far as is practicable, working in small parties of about 20 men under an officer.	CCO
Do.	21/7/15	6.30p.m.	Capt LANGMORE was wounded in the groin while marching out for night work on MENIN ROAD	CCO
Do.	22/7/15	6.30p.m.	One man was wounded while digging in the trenches. work was much hindered by heavy rain.	CCO
Do.	23/7/15	6.30p.m.	There was one casualty, wounded, during the night.	CCO
Do.	24/7/15		The working parties continued their work. The night passed off quietly	CCO
Do.	25/7/15		Instructions were received for the Batt'n to relieve the 10th Machine Gun Battery in H sector while the 2 Machine Guns belonging to the Batt'n on the night 26/27 July.	CCO
Do.	26/7/15	8.30p.m.	While inspecting the trenches Major HUGH ELLIOT Senior Major of the Batt'n was killed by a shell on the Cambridge CAMBRIDGE ROAD. Sergt. RICHARDS and the machine gun detachment went at 6.30p.m. to relieve the motor machine gun battery. Major ELLIOT's body was brought down from the dressing station of the 10th D.L.I. where it had been lying, and was buried at 10.p.m. that night. Sergt MOORE, who accompanied him to the trenches was wounded.	CCO Capt Hugh Shed 28A Magno Dysens TF Central.
Do.	27/7/15		Capt TROTTER was asked to go to the 43rd Batt Head Quarters to build huts for the H.Q. Mess and was granted permission to do so. There were no casualties among the working parties.	CCO
Do.	28/7/15		There were two casualties, wounded, among the working parties. One man was wounded, and another accidentally wounded. Lieut PAGET and the machine gun section have returned from the trenches.	CCO
Do.	29/7/15		The Batt'n formed a working (carrying) party for stores under Capt JOHNSON to the 42nd Inf'y Bde	CCO

Army Form C. 2118.

WAR DIARY
or
INTELLIGENCE SUMMARY.
(Erase heading not required.)

Instructions regarding War Diaries and Intelligence Summaries are contained in F. S. Regs., Part II. and the Staff Manual respectively. Title pages will be prepared in manuscript.

Place	Date	Hour	Summary of Events and Information	Remarks and references to Appendices
YPRES	30.7.15		One man was wounded when out with the working parties by day. No working parties went out the night there was a heavy bombardment during the day of the Enemy lines.	60
Do	31.7.15	7 p.m.	300 men under Capt BINGHAM were detailed as a carrying party for 42nd & 43rd Bns. Orders were received for the Battn to fall in and march to G.H.Q. line and to be placed at the disposal of the G.O.C. 43rd Bn. On arrival Lieut: Col: BAILEY temporarily took command of the Battn. He was ordered to take the Battn about 500 strong and report to the O.C. 10th D.L.I. at ZOUAVE WOOD I.18.c.6.2. in support of that Battn. A heavy bombardment was in progress all the time, and the Regt lost 1 killed and 2 wounded when leaving the LILLE GATE.	Capt hep shot 22.3.1mm

14th Division

12/7518

H.Y.
(20 sheets)

11th Kings Liverpool Rgt (Nineers)
Vol 4

Aug to Oct. 15

Confidential

War Diary

of

11th Bn Kings (Liverpool) Regiment (Pioneers)

from 1st August to 31st October.

N. J. Bailey Lt Col.
11th King's L'pool Regt (Pioneers)

WAR DIARY
INTELLIGENCE SUMMARY

Army Form C. 2118.

Place	Date	Hour	Summary of Events and Information	Remarks and references to Appendices
YPRES	1st Aug		The two companies in Sanctuary Wood trench in ZOUAVE WOOD. This work during the day began to clear a support trench in ZOUAVE WOOD. This work had to be stopped temporarily as the shelling of that portion of the ground became too heavy. Knife and wire made and brought up to the R.E. Officer in charge. Major Eyre received orders to withdraw to 2 Coy H.Q. army to B.H.Q. & take over a man & machine guns of the Somerset L.I. Infantry. The Companies arrived at their quarters billets at 11 p.m.	Mist.
	2nd Aug		At Headquarters Bde. they were detailed as carrying party for the 147th Brigade. The two Companies to T.H.Q. collected spades sandbags & spades for the Communication Trench on the South side. The trenches were shelled early in the morning slowly shelled again in the afternoon, when a good deal of the communication trench and Bde HQ lay at destroyed. This was all only reported that night. There was one casualty wounded. The remainder of the Bn. was at work that night repairing & lightening shooting trenches. Lt. Col. Barker again took over the duties of Brigadier temporarily.	Wet
	3rd Aug		Work was continued in repairing & improving existing Trenches & a front trench was dug from I'yd. 57. due South of then East to ZOUAVE WOOD. This was one casualty wounded. It was decided to establish at Divisional Armourers shop at Cleno in a branch of the Pioneer Workshop, in order to carry out extensive repairs to rifle, machine guns etc. without having to send them near to the Base. This shop is controlled by the O.C. 11th 13th the Kings (Spart'Yt) (Pioneer)	Wet
	4th Aug		All Coys. less two platoons continued trench work. Here two platoons were carrying casualties 1 Officer (2 Lt. Clayton) & two men wounded	Wet
	5th Aug		Short Sharp bombardment by Germans about 3am & 4 am. One officer 2nd Lt. Gray slightly wounded. The Battalion continued digging & repairing trenches at night.	Wet
	6th Aug		Short sharp Bombardment by Germans about 3am to 4am. The weather had continued causing & repairing trenches at night. However & casualties.	

Army Form C. 2118.

WAR DIARY
or
INTELLIGENCE SUMMARY.
(Erase heading not required.)

Instructions regarding War Diaries and Intelligence Summaries are contained in F. S. Regs., Part II. and the Staff Manual respectively. Title pages will be prepared in manuscript.

Place	Date	Hour	Summary of Events and Information	Remarks and references to Appendices
YPRES	Aug 7th		Short but sharp Bombardment by Germans about 2.a.m. to 3.a.m, and again from 4.p.m to 5.h.P.M. The Battalion did not go out at night. One man killed and three wounded in YPRES.	V.D.S.
	" 8th		Bombardment by Germans, no working parties out on account of the Battn standing to in Reserve.	V.D.S.
	" 9th	3.30 AM	Bombardment attack early in the morning. The Battalion stood to in Reserve all day. At night "C" Coy moved up in support into dug-outs South of the MENIN Road (I.9.a.5.5.) Sheet 28.1.20,000. "A" Coy as a carrying party. B & D Coys repaired trenches (communication). C Coy returned	V.D.S.
	" 10th		"A" Coy acted as a carrying party. B & D Coys dug & repaired Trenches. C Coy returned to Billets at 10.P.M.	
	" 11th	6.P.M.	B, D, Coys & one Platoon of C Coy digging & repairing Trenches at night. The remainder of the Battalion acted as carrying parties.	V.D.S.
	" 12th	7.a.m.	Heavy Bombardment of YPRES Cathedral. About 2.6. men of the 5th D.C.L.I. were buried under the debris of the Cloisters which had fallen in. The Battalion sent down a rescue party, at the arrival another shell landed five of this party & wounded nine. Another one, shortly after their arrival, went down & succeeded in eventually recovering four men alive & the rescue party immediately went down & carried out the 3.P.M. In connection with this the following N.C.O.'s the last of whom was not released until 3.P.M. In connection with this the G.O.C. 14th Division-in No.12637. Capt H. Murray, No. 19296 a/C.S. Shilling, No 9812 Pte L. Kenmare and No. 13694. a/C. J Cook. Many were to recently brought to the notice of the G.O.C. 14th Division-V3 No.	V.D.13.
	" 13th		Three more bodies of the 5th D.C.L.I. were recovered from beneath the ruins of the Cathedral & were buried alongside those of the previous day in the cemetery by the Prison. The Battalion continued digging and repairing Trenches	V.D.S
	" 14th		The Battalion continued digging and renovating Trenches	V.D.S
	" 15th		The Battalion continued digging and renovating trenches	V.D.S

WAR DIARY
INTELLIGENCE SUMMARY

(Erase heading not required.)

Army Form C. 2118.

Instructions regarding War Diaries and Intelligence Summaries are contained in F. S. Regs., Part II. and the Staff Manual respectively. Title pages will be prepared in manuscript.

Place	Date	Hour	Summary of Events and Information	Remarks and references to Appendices
YPRES	16th May		The Battalion continued digging & repairing trenches. There were no casualties.	
	17th May		The Battalion continued digging & repairing trenches. There were no casualties.	
	18th May		The Battalion continued digging & repairing trenches. There was no casualties.	
	19 Aug		It was decided to build dugouts on account of the safety of billet being inadequate. Half the Battalion dug out dugouts whilst the remainder worked at night digging & repairing trenches & dugouts.	
	20th May		Half the Battalion continued making dugouts whilst the remainder dug & repaired trenches. There were no casualties.	
	21st "		Half the Battalion continued digging dugouts & the other half Battalion dug & repaired trenches at night. No casualties.	
	22nd "		Half the Battalion continued digging dugouts & the other half Battalion were digging & repairing trenches. No casualties.	
	23rd "		Half the Battalion continued digging dugouts & the other half Battalion were digging & repairing trenches. No casualties.	
	24th "		Half the Battalion continued digging dugouts & the other half Battalion were digging & repairing trenches. No casualties.	
	25th "		Half the Battalion continued digging dugouts & the other half Battalion were digging & repairing trenches. No casualties.	
	26th "		Half the Battalion continued digging dugouts & the other half Battalion were digging & repairing trenches. Casualties 1 killed 2 wounded.	killed

Army Form C. 2118.

WAR DIARY
INTELLIGENCE SUMMARY.
(Erase heading not required.)

Instructions regarding War Diaries and Intelligence Summaries are contained in F. S. Regs., Part II. and the Staff Manual respectively. Title pages will be prepared in manuscript.

Place	Date	Hour	Summary of Events and Information	Remarks and references to Appendices
YPRES	August 27th		Half the Battalion continued digging and repairing trenches, whilst the other half continued working dug-outs. No casualties.	V.J.13.
	Aug 28th		,,	V.J.13.
	,, 29th		,,	V.J.13.
	,, 30th		,,	V.J.13.
	,, 31st		,,	V.J.13.

Army Form C. 2118.

WAR DIARY
INTELLIGENCE SUMMARY.
(Erase heading not required.)

Instructions regarding War Diaries and Intelligence
Summaries are contained in F. S. Regs., Part II.
and the Staff Manual respectively. Title pages
will be prepared in manuscript.

Place	Date	Hour	Summary of Events and Information	Remarks and references to Appendices
YPRES.	Sept 1st	10 a.m.	Half the Battalion continued digging & repairing Trenches whilst the remainder continued making dug-outs. A short bombardment by the Germans of Ypres. The Battalion had Six N.C.O.'s & men wounded.	1/9/13.
"	2nd	11 a.m.	Half the Battalion continued digging & repairing Trenches, the remainder making dug-outs. A short but sharp bombardment by the Enemy.	2/9/13.
"	3rd	6 p.m.	Half the Battalion continued digging & repairing Trenches, the remainder continued work on the dug-outs. One man wounded.	3/9/13.
"	the 4.		Half the Battalion continued digging & renovating Trenches, the remainder continued work on the dug-outs. Ypres again bombarded for a short time.	4/9/13.

WAR DIARY
~~INTELLIGENCE~~ SUMMARY.
(Erase heading not required.)

Army Form C. 2118.

Place	Date	Hour	Summary of Events and Information	Remarks and references to Appendices
YPRES	Sep 5th		Half the Battalion continued making dug outs whilst the other half repaired trenches which were in very bad condition after 36 hours continuous rain.	
YPRES	Sep 6th		Half the Battalion continued making dug outs whilst the other half repaired trenches.	
"	"		At 9am heavy shelling of the trenches by the German artillery. Bullets escape dug out by Pts Hill Coy Sgt S Cartery Rarn & others. Our Battalion continued digging & repairing trenches. There were no casualties.	
"	Sep 7th		Casualties: Battalion continued digging & repairing trenches. One man wounded.	
"	Sep 8th		Half the Battalion digging & repairing trenches, the remainder working	
"	Sep 9th		dug outs. 150 men were also assisting R.E. digging trenches. One man wounded	
"	Sep 10th		Half the Battalion digging & repairing trenches. The remainder were assisting R.E. No casualties.	
"	Sep 11th		Half Battalion digging & repairing trenches. Remainder working on dug outs same as yesterday. Approx 200 total casualties. Also 100 men were sent on working party. Also 100 men repairing trenches at night.	
"	Sep 12th		Half the Battalion digging & repairing trenches in the day, the remainder working on dug outs. Two killed & 4 wounded.	
"	Sep 13th		Half the Battalion digging & repairing trenches by day & to dug outs working in dug outs repairing trenches by day & working on dug outs by night. There were no casualties.	

WAR DIARY or INTELLIGENCE SUMMARY.

(Erase heading not required.)

Army Form C. 2118.

Place	Date	Hour	Summary of Events and Information	Remarks and references to Appendices
YPRES	Apr 14th		Half the Battalion digging & repairing trenches at night, the remainder working in trenches by day also dugouts. There were no casualties. Hr Gen J. met Report from HT Corps.	Wed
"	15th		Half the Battalion digging and repairing trenches at night, the remainder in trenches by day & dugouts. Inspection of half front by Corps Commander. Capt. Brown D. Hall having proceeded on leave.	Wed
"	16th		Half the Battalion digging & repairing trenches at night. Completing dugouts for Battalion two reserve trenches by day; a small party on dugouts, Major Hilly McKinley & Lieut Gill. Lt. Mulvey returned from leave. Lieut Ord slightly wounded.	Wed
"	17th		Three companies out at night repairing & digging trenches, two platoons out repairing trenches by day, one platoon out & Service Signal Co the remainder on Battalion dugouts. No Casualties.	Wed
"	18th		Three companies out at night repairing trenches by day, one platoon, two platoons out repairing trenches by day, one platoon last at Service Signal Co, the remainder on Battalion dugouts. No Casualties.	Wed
"	19th		Three companies out at night repairing & digging trenches, two platoons out repairing trenches by day, one platoon with a Service Signal Co the remainder on Battalion dugouts. No Casualties.	Wed
"	20th		Three companies out at night repairing & digging trenches, two platoons out repairing trenches by day, one platoon with a Service Signal Co the remainder on Battalion dugouts.	Wed

Army Form C. 2118.

WAR DIARY
or
INTELLIGENCE SUMMARY.
(Erase heading not required.)

Instructions regarding War Diaries and Intelligence Summaries are contained in F. S. Regs., Part II. and the Staff Manual respectively. Title pages will be prepared in manuscript.

Place	Date	Hour	Summary of Events and Information	Remarks and references to Appendices
YPRES	21st Sept		Three Companies out digging & repairing trenches at night, few platoon at repairing trenches by day, one platoon with 14 Division Signal Company, the remainder in Battalion dugouts. No Casualties.	M.S.
"	22nd		Three Companies out digging & repairing trenches at night, few platoon at repairing trenches by day, one platoon with 14 Division Signal Company, the remainder in Battalion dugouts. No casualties. No men wounded.	M.S.
"	23rd		Three Companies at night repairing trenches, one platoon by day, one platoon with 14 Division Signal Company. At repairing trenches by day, one platoon with 14 Division Signal Company. The remainder in Battalion dugouts.	M.S.
"	24th		Two platoons in trenches during day repairing. Battalion standing to, commencement of attack, small parties in trenches all night repairing. 2nd Lt Eddy wounded & 2 men.	M.S.
"	25th		Battalion standing to. Heavy bombardment about 11 am. Parties in trenches all day long, keeping same in repair. Casualties 3 wounded. Lt Pl Snetzinger and one knight and 1 Sergeant to the work.	M.S.
"	26th		Battalion feed-out day parties in trenches also parties to trenches dead, worked on dug-outs & generally cleared up sheet of debris. Casualties 2nd Lt Malloy & 4 other ranks wounded.	M.S.
YPRES				

Army Form C. 2118.

WAR DIARY
or
INTELLIGENCE SUMMARY.
(Erase heading not required.)

Instructions regarding War Diaries and Intelligence Summaries are contained in F. S. Regs., Part II. and the Staff Manual respectively. Title pages will be prepared in manuscript.

Place	Date	Hour	Summary of Events and Information	Remarks and references to Appendices
YPRES	Sept 27th		Two Companies worked by night on Communication Trenches, & about 70 more by day. The remainder of the Battalion continued work on Dug-outs and making Trench materials. A short Bombardment in the evening by the Enemy.	V.J.13.
	28th	6 P.M.	Two Companies worked by night on trenches & about 70 men by day. The remainder of the Battalion on dug-outs & making Trench materials. One man wounded. The Brigade Hd. Qrs. on Ramparts damaged by 17" shell & 2 men buried unburnt debris. We sent men to rescue those burned. Pr. Smith invalided home sick.	V.J.13.
	29th		Two Companies worked by night on trenches & about 70 men by day. The remainder of the Battalion on dug-outs & Trench materials. Six men wounded, and 3 men killed. Casualties — Pr. L. Whittaker & 2 men wounded.	V.J.13.
	30th		Three Companies continued work on the Trenches by day & night. The remaining Company worked on dug-outs & making Trench materials. No casualties.	V.J.13.

Army Form C. 2118.

WAR DIARY
or
INTELLIGENCE SUMMARY.
(Erase heading not required.)

Instructions regarding War Diaries and Intelligence Summaries are contained in F. S. Regs., Part II. and the Staff Manual respectively. Title pages will be prepared in manuscript.

Place	Date	Hour	Summary of Events and Information	Remarks and references to Appendices
YPRES.	Oct 1st		Three Companies continued work on Communication Trenches by day & night, the remaining Coy worked on dug-outs, and supplied a party for tunnelling work on Ramparts under Capt French 5th K.S.L.I.	V.D.W.
"	2nd		" "	V.D.W.
"	3rd		Three Companies worked on Trenches by day & night. The remainder worked on dug-outs, tunnelling work on Ramparts, & also supplied men for work in erecting huts under supervision of the Royal Engineers. One man wounded.	V.D.W.

WAR DIARY
or
INTELLIGENCE SUMMARY.
(Erase heading not required.)

Army Form C. 2118.

Place	Date	Hour	Summary of Events and Information	Remarks and references to Appendices
YPRES October	4th		Three companies worked day & night on communication trenches the remaining Company are spelt up to parties working for the Engineers about trench.	Ed.
"	Oct 5th		Three companies worked by day & night on communication trenches, the remaining Company was split up into parties working for the Engineers. Capt Though Connolly & Cpl Connolly (wounded) 2nd Lt (J.B.) TISDALE was assisted by Kelly, Jones & Bell. Communication.	Ed.
"	Oct 6th		Three companies. The remaining Company was split up into parties working for the Engineers. Two dug-outs for infantry were started. 2nd Lt CHADWICK joined the Batt'n. One casual (y.) (wounded)	Ed.
"	Oct 7th		Three companies at work by day & night on communication trenches, emergency fire trenches & new trench F. Being made off 2 communication trenches, & new trench F. Being dug. One Company providing parties under R.E. on railways, under the Bde Mining Section, or working parties under at GOODACRE. & working on the RAMPARTS.	Ed.
"	Oct 8		The four companies were at work as yesterday. One casualty (killed).	Ed.
"	Oct 9th		Four companies at work as yesterday. Rather heavy shelling in YPRES at times.	Ed.

WAR DIARY
or
INTELLIGENCE SUMMARY.

(Erase heading not required.)

Army Form C. 2118.

Instructions regarding War Diaries and Intelligence Summaries are contained in F. S. Regs., Part II. and the Staff Manual respectively. Title pages will be prepared in manuscript.

Place	Date	Hour	Summary of Events and Information	Remarks and references to Appendices
YPRES.	Oct 10th		Three companies at work by day & night on the communication trenches. One company providing parties for R.E. mining, Railways, Dugouts at the Ramparts. Special message from Major General Cooper to the Battn. on its work attached.	Appd.
"	Oct 11		Four Companies at work as yesterday. Some 17" shells in YPRES about 9-10 am. One man wounded.	Appd.
"	Oct 12.		Four Companies at work as yesterday.	Appd.
"	Oct 13.		The usual Company on by day providing various parties. Owing to heavy shelling of YPRES from 6.30 p.m. - 10.0 p.m. only one company proceeded to work at night, on MUD LANE. A horse in the town was set on fire.	Appd.
"	Oct 14		Three companies worked on communication trenches by day and one company provided usual fatigues for R.E. & dugouts. No casualty.	Appd.
"	Oct 15th		Three companies worked on communication trenches by day and one Company provided usual fatigues for R.E. dugouts etc. Foggy most of the day but no Whitley so fairly peaceful	Appd.
"	Oct 16		Three companies worked on communication trenches by day & one company provided usual fatigues for R.E. dugouts etc. Rifle fire in morning.	Appd.
"	Oct 17.		Three Companies worked on communication trenches by day & one Company provided usual fatigues for R.E. dugouts etc. the shelling by in the morning. Position peaceable. One casualty wounded.	Appd.

WAR DIARY
or
INTELLIGENCE SUMMARY.

(Erase heading not required.)

Army Form C. 2118.

Place	Date	Hour	Summary of Events and Information	Remarks and references to Appendices
	Oct 18th		Three Companies worked on trenches by day. Taylor One Company provided night parties, parties working with R.E. General fatigues. The Casualty Nominal.	
	Oct 19th		Three Companies worked on Trenches by day employed on Company provided night parties, parties working with R.E & General fatigues	
	Oct 20th		Three Companies worked on trenches by day employed. One Company provided Night parties, parties working with R.E General fatigues. No men wounded.	
	Oct 21st		Battalion received orders to move billets to rest. Only day parties proceeded to trenches.	
	Oct 22nd		The Battalion marched by Coy. from from 9. a.m. to ... proceeded to Steenvoorde. There it entrained for POPERINGHE arrived there at 11.15 a.m. detrained & marched to WATON BILLET in the vicinity	
	Oct 23rd		The Commanding Officer inspected Billets in the morning. Some platoon drill till 9am, the remainder of the day was taken up in cleaning equipment etc.	

Army Form C. 2118.

WAR DIARY
or
INTELLIGENCE SUMMARY.
(Erase heading not required.)

Instructions regarding War Diaries and Intelligence Summaries are contained in F. S. Regs., Part II. and the Staff Manual respectively. Title pages will be prepared in manuscript.

Place	Date	Hour	Summary of Events and Information	Remarks and references to Appendices
WATOU	Oct 24th		Church Parade in the morning. Companies practised football in the afternoon.	Wd
"	Oct 25th	7.3.	Section drill before breakfast. Remainder of the day	Wd
"	Oct 26th	9, 12	Section drill, Platoon drill by all Companies. Plans for platoon instruction the Battalion at work in the morning. In the afternoon the rest of the time was spent in playing games.	Wd
"	Oct 27th	2-3p	Rain in the morning. Lt Col Busby, Capt + Adj of Eastbourne To Reynolds. Sergeant Major + 25 other ranks of the Battalion formed an escort of His Composite Battalion representing 14th Senior Corps, which was inspected by His Majesty the King accompanied by the Army Commander. The remainder of the Battalion route marched in the morning.	Wd
"	Oct 28th		The Battalion carried on its training although the weather was much against outdoor work.	Wd
"	Oct 29th		The Battalion route marched in the morning	Wd

1577 Wt.W10791/1773 500,000 1/15 D. D. & L. A.D.S.S./Forms/C. 2118.

Army Form C. 2118.

WAR DIARY
INTELLIGENCE SUMMARY.
(Erase heading not required.)

Instructions regarding War Diaries and Intelligence Summaries are contained in F. S. Regs., Part II. and the Staff Manual respectively. Title pages will be prepared in manuscript.

Place	Date	Hour	Summary of Events and Information	Remarks and references to Appendices
WATOU	Oct 30th		On this date the Baths were allotted to the Battalion so no work was done.	
"	Oct 31st		The weather being very bad no church parade was held. In the afternoon "A" Company played "B" Company in the second round of the Inter Company football match. The result was a draw of two goals each. The Commanding Officer presented a bass for gallantry to Cpl Hartogue of "C" Company.	Aud.

Copy of Message from Major General Couper

"I am very pleased with the way all the Officers, N.C.O's and men of your Battalion have been working, and I am sure that you will like to know that I have heard about this work from all Units of the Division over and above what I have seen with my own eyes.
This work refers not only to the trenches, but also to the work in the shops. The whole work of your Battalion has been excellent."

(Sgd) V. Couper.
Major General.

10.10.15.

5.Y.
(7 sheets)

11th Liverpool
vol. 5

121/7635

14th Wreck

Nov. 15

K

Registered

Confidential

War Diary.

of

11th Bt. King's Liverpool Regiment (Pioneers)

from 1st November to 30th November

1915.

Volume 6.

Army Form C. 2118.

WAR DIARY
or
INTELLIGENCE SUMMARY.

(Erase heading not required.)

Instructions regarding War Diaries and Intelligence Summaries are contained in F.S. Regs., Part II. and the Staff Manual respectively. Title pages will be prepared in manuscript.

Place	Date	Hour	Summary of Events and Information	Remarks and references to Appendices
WATOU	Nov 1	7.30 am 6-8 9-12.30	Physical drill. The Battalion carried on with the programme of training. In the afternoon it poured with rain. Rained all day, only lectures could be carried out.	
"	Nov 2		"	
"	Nov 3	7.30 am 9.30 9-12.30	Section Drill before breakfast. Route March of about 8 miles the early part of the weather was very little better in the afternoon. Lt. F. W. Whittaker left the Battalion sponsored Carried out in Musketry to join the 1/5 R. Sussex. [Company].	
"	Nov 4	7.30-8 9 am 11.30-12.30 2-3	Physical Drill. Examination by Company Commanders of their Section leaders. Musketry in General Drill & C.S.M. Ramsdale was severely wounded with [illegible] instructors in bomb throwing. All officers were instructed in the use of Bombing.	
"	Nov 5	7.30 am 9-12 2-3	Section drill. Route march of about 8 miles. Lectures by officers. The day was extremely fine, we went at all forms of outdoor training.	
"	Nov 6	7-8 9-12	Physical Drill Commanding Officers inspection.	
"	Nov 7	11 am	Church Parade. Football was played in the afternoon.	

WAR DIARY
or
INTELLIGENCE SUMMARY.

(Erase heading not required.)

Army Form C. 2118.

Place	Date	Hour	Summary of Events and Information	Remarks and references to Appendices
WATOU	Nov 8th	7.30 9-12.30 2-3p	Physical Drill Company, Platoon, Section drill, Bomb throwing & machine gun instruction Manual & Musketry Drill	Fwd.
"	Nov 9	7.30-8 9.30 6 1.30	Physical Drill Route March of about 10 miles.	do Fwd.
"	Nov 10	7.30-8 9-12.30 2-3	Physical Drill Company, Platoon, Section drill Musketry in General	do Fwd.
"	Nov 11	7.30-8 9-12.30	Physical Drill Company Platoon, Section drill. Bomb throwing and machine gun instruction	Fwd.
"	Nov 12	7.30-8 9-12.30 2-3.30	No drill was possible, poured with rain all day. No work of any description was pursued with the exception of lecture to Officers	Fwd.
"	Nov 13	9.12.30	All training was carried on indoors, the weather was too bad to allow of any outdoor training.	
"	Nov 14	11.30	Church Parade.	
"	Nov 15th	7.30-8 9-12	Physical Drill. Centre Platoon Drill, Bomb throwing, machine gun instruction, Major Gen. & Company Commanders went to view some German trenches. One casualty, accidentally killed during course of bomb instruction.	

WAR DIARY
or
INTELLIGENCE SUMMARY.

Army Form C. 2118.

Place	Date	Hour	Summary of Events and Information	Remarks and references to Appendices
WATOU	Nov 16		Several Bath. were allotted to the Battalion for the day	Shel
		7.30	Physical drill	
		9-1	Route March	
		2-3p	Inspection of feet	
"	Nov 18	7.30-8	Physical Drill	Shel
		9-12.30	Musketry, Platoon & Section drill	
"	Nov 19	9.1.30	Packing up prior to moving back to rest quarters	Shel
		3.30	Left Watou for Poperinghe. Marching	
		5.30	Arrived at Poperinghe entrained arriving at YPRES 7pm & proceeded to Old Bilge where we were taken into new sector	
YPRES	Nov 20		Officers reconnoitred new sector	Shel
"	Nov 21	10am	Church Parade	Shel
		5.30pm	Sector (ST JEAN) in communication trenches. 3 Companies proceeded to work in new workshops, drying rooms, dugouts. One Company worked for Battalion dugouts, workshops, etc.	
"	Nov 22		This day was spent up on this day. One Company found parties for Battalion dugouts, workshops. Hastings for collection of wood, & repair of paths	Shel
"	Nov 23	5.30pm	Three Companies proceeded with work on Communication Trenches. One company found parties for Battalion dugouts, workshops, fatigues. 3 parties of French tramways. Three companies worked on communication trenches. Two casualties.	Shel
"	Nov 24		One company found parties for Battalion dugouts, workshops, fatigues. Three companies worked on communication trenches.	Shel
		5.30pm	parties on French tramways. There were no casualties	
"	Nov 25		By day & night the Coy. company found parties. My Battalion dugouts. Three companies worked on communication trenches parties on French tramways.	Shel
"	Nov 26		Duties by day & night found parties for Battalion dugouts, workshops, fatigues. One Company. Three companies worked on communication trenches.	Shel
		5.30pm	parties on French tramways. There were no casualties	

WAR DIARY
or
INTELLIGENCE SUMMARY.
(Erase heading not required.)

Army Form C. 2118.

Place	Date	Hour	Summary of Events and Information	Remarks and references to Appendices
YPRES	Nov 27		One Company found parties for Battalion dugouts, workshops, fatigue four parties on trench tramways. Three companies worked by night on communication trenches. There were no casualties.	G.60.8
"	Nov 28		One Company found parties for Battalion dugouts, workshops, fatigue four parties on trench tramways. Three companies worked by day on communication trenches.	G.60.8
		10 am	Church Parade.	
"	Nov 29		One Company found parties for Battalion dugouts, workshops & fatigues, four parties on trench tramways. Three companies worked by night on communication trenches. No casualties.	G.60.8
		5.30 pm		
"	Nov 30		One Company found parties for Battalion dugouts, workshops & fatigues, four parties on trench tramways. Three companies worked by day & night on communication trenches. Casualties. Two wounded. Three new officers joined on night of 29/30. 2nd Lieuts Sorge, Christie & Beckwith-Yonge.	V.4.S.

6.Y.
(8 sheets)

<u>Confidential</u>

War Diary

of

11th Bn King's Liverpool Regt (Pioneers)

From 1st December 1915 to 31st December 1915.

(Volume. 7.)

Army Form C. 2118.

WAR DIARY
or
INTELLIGENCE SUMMARY.
(Erase heading not required.)

Place	Date	Hour	Summary of Events and Information	Remarks and references to Appendices
YPRES	Dec 1st		One company found parties for Battalion dugouts, workshops, four parties on Trench Tramways. Three companies worked by day & night on Communication trenches. There were no casualties.	Glad.
YPRES	Dec 2nd		One Company found parties for Battalion dugouts, workshops, fatigues, four parties on Trench Tramways. Three companies worked by day & night on Communication trenches. There were two casualties wounded. 2nd Lt R.B. SALT & one Other Rank.	Glad.
"	Dec 3rd		One Company found parties for Battalion dugouts workshops fatigues & four parties on Trench Tramways. Three companies worked by day & night on Communication trenches. There were no casualties.	GNS
"	Dec 4th		One Company found parties for Battalion dugouts, workshops, fatigues & four parties on Trench Tramways. Three companies worked by day & night on Communication trenches for Battalion dugouts, workshops, fatigue & night on Communication trenches. No casualties.	Glad.
"	Dec 5th		One Company found parties for Battalion dugouts, workshops, fatigues & four parties on Trench Tramways. Three companies worked by day & night on Communication trenches. 2nd BATES & Cpl. H.W. WHITE R.A.M.C. & QM CALLAGHAN & one man wounded.	Glad.
"	Dec 6th		During shelled very heavily for an hour & three dugouts were damaged. One Company found parties for Battalion dugouts, workshops, & four parties on Trench Tramways. Three companies worked by day & night. There were no casualties.	Glad.
"	Dec 7th		Communication trenches by day & night. One Company found parties for Battalion dugouts, workshops, fatigues & four parties on Trench Tramways. Three companies worked on Communication trenches, 2nd Lt. E. Austin joined. Felt in the evening 7.65.	

Army Form C. 2118.

WAR DIARY
or
INTELLIGENCE SUMMARY.
(Erase heading not required.)

Instructions regarding War Diaries and Intelligence Summaries are contained in F. S. Regs., Part II. and the Staff Manual respectively. Title pages will be prepared in manuscript.

Place	Date	Hour	Summary of Events and Information	Remarks and references to Appendices
YPRES	Dec 8th		One Company found parties for Battalion dugouts, workshops fatigues & four parties on Trench tramways. Three Companies worked on Communication trenches by day & night. There were no Casualties.	Shel.
"	Dec 9th		One Company found parties for Battalion, dugouts, workshops fatigues, & four parties on Trench tramways. Three Companies worked on Communication trenches by day & night. There were No casualties but not sufficient parties to relieve the Battalion	Shel.
"	Dec 10th		One Company found parties for Battalion, dugouts, workshops fatigues & four parties on Trench tramways. Three Companies worked on Communication trenches by day & night for the wounded & four casualties but not of sufficient party for the wounded to leave the Battalion.	Shel.
"	Dec 11th		One Company found parties for Battalion dugouts, workshops fatigues & four parties on Trench tramways. Three Companies worked on Communication trenches by day & night. There were no Casualties.	Shel.
"	Dec 16th		One Company found parties for Battalion, dugouts, workshops fatigues & four parties on Trench tramways. Three Companies worked on Communication trenches by day & night. There was no Casualty.	Shel.

WAR DIARY
or
INTELLIGENCE SUMMARY.
(Erase heading not required.)

Army Form C. 2118.

Place	Date	Hour	Summary of Events and Information	Remarks and references to Appendices
YPRES	Dec 13th		One Company found parties for Battalion dugouts, fatigue & pipe parties but the remainder of three Companies worked on Embankment Trenches by day & night. Second Lieut C.G. Bredman & 10 O. Ranks wounded. 2 O. Ranks killed	Ref.
"	Dec 14th		The Battalion received orders to move to WATOU on 15th inst. One Company has employed on starting trench mortars & in general preparing for move off. B Coy proceeded to work at night, there were no casualties.	Ref.
YPRES	Dec 15th	8.30	Transport moved off. Also Companies by platoons. Entrained at YLAMERTINGHE for POPERINGHE thence WATOU. The Battalion accomplished its	Ref.
WATOU		10.30 a.m.		
		1.15 p.m.	march route to WATOU. There were no casualties.	
	Dec 16th	9 a.m.	General inspection of clothing & kits by Company Officers	Ref.
"		11.30	Half transport formed & 61st R.E. Fatigue detachment	
			General instruction in Pigeots, outposts, sentries & extension	
"	Dec 17th	9 a.m.	meter.	
		12.30	Lost their instruction in Pigeots. Battalion joined the Battalion	Ref.
		2-3	General instruction in Pigeots, outposts, sentries & extended order	
"	Dec 18th	9 a.m.	drill. The following message from the G.O.C. of the 2nd DIVISION was received	
"			"The G.O.C. has been told by all the 3 Brigadiers of the excellent & willing work done by the Officers & men of the Bt[n] in their various sectors during the last month. The G.O.C. is very pleased but in no way surprised to receive those reports knowing the way in which the Battalion has worked since they came under his Command"	Ref.

Army Form C. 2118.

WAR DIARY
or
INTELLIGENCE SUMMARY.
(Erase heading not required.)

Instructions regarding War Diaries and Intelligence Summaries are contained in F. S. Regs., Part II. and the Staff Manual respectively. Title pages will be prepared in manuscript.

Place	Date	Hour	Summary of Events and Information	Remarks and references to Appendices
WATOU	Dec 19th	7 am	Orders from the Division to attend to or account if an attack	
"		12 Noon	Orders received to hold ourselves in readiness to proceed to POPERINGHE	
"		2 pm	Orders received that Battalion need stand to no longer, for attack had failed.	Ypres
"	Dec 20th	9.0	Company's carried out training in Outposts, Guards, Such is it.	Ypres
		2-3	Lectures in entraining & entrustation.	
"	Dec 21st	9-12	Route March. Her outdoor work. Musketry & lecture carried out under Company arrangements.	Ypres
"	Dec 22nd	6-7.30	During the morning a student order drill.	Ypres
		1-3	Baths were allotted 6th Battalion	
"	Dec 23rd	6-10	Physical drill	
		10-11	Company drill	
		11-12	Extended order	
		2-3	OC Companies lectured their Officers, Company streled under Company Sergeant Majors.	Ypres
"	Dec 24th	9-10	Physical Drill	
		10-11	Saluting order drill	
		11-12	Outposts Sentries, Guards, Musketry	
		2-3	Lecture & Company drill	
		7.30 pm	Draft of 40 arrived.	
"	Dec 25th		Xmas Day.	
"	Dec 26th		All orders with regard to the move behind SOMAR recently received	Ypres
		11.30 am	very cancelled.	
			Men Church Parade	

WAR DIARY
or
INTELLIGENCE SUMMARY.

(Erase heading not required.)

Army Form C. 2118.

Place	Date	Hour	Summary of Events and Information	Remarks and references to Appendices
WATOU	DEC 27th	9-10	Physical Drill	
		10-11a	Company Drill	
		11-12a	Musketry Instruction by Platoon commanders to former Sec.	SheS
		2-3pm	Route March	
WATOU	Dec 28	9-12.30	Platoon Drill	
		2-3 pm		
WATOU	Dec 29	9-10	Physical Drill	
		10-12	Extended Order	
		2-3	Platoon Drill	
			Orders were received that the Battalion would move to the trenches on 31st. Four machine guns forwarded to trenches. Capt Yettes Lt Stanton & 40 men proceeded to the new workshops	SheS
WATOU	Dec 30th	9-10	Physical Drill	
		10-11	Company drill	
		11-12	Kit inspection	
		2-3	Smoke helmet inspection	
			General preparation for move	
WATOU	Dec 31	9-11	All orders for move were cancelled & fresh orders issued.	
		11.30	Preparation for move on move to ELVERDINGHE for this Companies one Company 13 Coy provided by motor	SheS
		6 pm	Arrived ELVERDINGHE CHATEAU. 13 Coy provided by motor lorry to Canal Bank.	
ELVERDINGHE	Jan 1st		Reconnaissance of Trenches by OC Coys who were to move & Much...	JP

14th Division

ORDERLY ROOM
A 618
21 DEC 1915
11th (Service) Bn. The King's L'pool Rgt.

In accordance with 14th Div R.O.
No 1029 dated 18-12-15.
Amendments to Battalion Roll.

No	Rank & name	Coy	Remarks
3/1115 8	Pte Steging H	"D"	Evacuated out of Div area 20-12-15. & struck off the strength
13854	Pte Hill	B	Admitted to Hospital 20-12-15.
12031	" Fox	A	" " " 20-12-15.
12155	" Bradley	A	Discharged from Hospital 20-12-15.

21-12-15.

E. C. Ogle Major
Commanding

11th (S) Bn. The King's Liverpool Regt. (Pioneers)

14th Division

Return in accordance with 14th Division Routine Order No. 1029 dated 18.12.15

11th (S) Bn. The King's Liverpool Regt. (Pioneers)

No	Rank	Name	Coy	Remarks	No	Rank	Name	Coy	Rmks
12114	Cpl	Ainscough H.	a		20811	Pte	Ballen F.	a	
20825	Pte	Atkinson W	a		12023	.	Balmforth W	.	
20845	.	Allman J.	.		3/11875	.	Bailey J.	.	
12317	.	Allen J.D.	.		16480	.	Bowness P.	.	
12119	Sgt	Abbott J	.		3/10975	L/C	Bramwell F.	.	
12013	Pte	Allport A	.		12992	Pte	Black M.	.	
25608	.	Anderson J	B	Hospital	26710	.	Brading CF	.	
14156	.	Anness L	.		12732	Cpl	Burrows J	B	
20839	.	Allcock H	.		8757	L/C	Butler M.	.	
9468	.	Aird P	.		12209	Pte	Balmer J	.	
25907	.	Avis J	.		11856	.	Banks H	.	
12390	Sgt	Anderson F.	C		12495	.	Barker W	.	
12953	Pte	Abrahams M.	.		12743	.	Barrett R	.	Hospital
12927	.	Allen J	.		12375	.	Baynes B	.	
12568	.	Adkins W	.		12789	.	Beatty J	.	
18240	.	Anderson R	.		18011	.	Blackstone J	.	
27781	.	Andrews W.	D		13312	.	Bell H	.	
14157	.	Archbold W	.		9280	.	Bell R	.	
12336	.	Allen J	.		12964	.	Boyer W	.	
12974	.	Armstrong W	.		12965	.	Brooks F	.	
13108	.	Adlington A	.	Hospital	12971	.	Brough W	.	
13220	.	Almond A	.		20471	.	Brennan W	.	
21218	.	Anderson L	.		21208	.	Brown W	.	
					23754	.	Brown J	.	
7142	L/C	Bostock G	a		12298	.	Byron J	.	
13943	Sgt	Booth B	.		8892	.	Bonell W	.	
12089	Pte	Blair R	.		2620	.	Blair D	.	
20761	.	Barton J	.		25125	.	Barnett J	.	
12005	Cpl	Bradley J	.		28051	.	Brennan J	.	
12024	Pte	Bradley A	a		14529	.	Brennan J	.	
12155	.	Bradley E	.	Hospital	25863	.	Brigden H	.	
12030	.	Budden W	.		12115	.	Barton J	.	
12032	L/C	Burgess G	.		12366	Sgt	Burke J	C	
12637	"	Bowles J	.		18052	Cpl	Boocock C	.	
12175	Pte	Buckles J	.		12859	Pte	Bond E	.	
12448	.	Burns L	.		13042	.	Bryce W	.	
25625	.	Bawden C	.		12708	.	Brereton A	.	
3/11315	.	Baines W	.		20747	.	Bradford F	.	
12093	.	Brown P	.		21241	.	Bancroft J	.	
12152	.	Beattie H	.		20844	.	Burke C	.	

11th (S) Bn. The King's Liverpool Regt. (Pioneers)

No.	Rank & Name		Coy	Remarks	No.	Rank & Name		Coy	Remks
12599	Pte	Ball. W.	C		12484	L/C	Corness G.	B	
21132		Boardman. J.			12850		Cassidy C		
20899		Brady. W			12279	Pte	Carberry W		
12325		Ball. W			12727		Carlson H		
13122		Beggs J			10353		Carney W		
18932		Brown H.C			21196		Carlyle R		
9342	Cpl	Blundell W.			18072		Carrick W		
12534	Pte	Broulsford Q		Hospital	21243		Carter W		
28052		Brown E			26765		Carter A		
20821		Bradshaw J			12241		Cartledge J		
26289		Bamber W			25605		Cartwright J		
13849		Bevan J			12892		Clarke J		
12797		Brannigan C			12301		Collins W		
12826		Brearley L	D		12822		Cannell C		
8955		Bradley J			12254		Conway J		
10142		Barnfather S			13144		Coolson J		
25108		Bibby J			20824		Cooke J		
8095		Burns M			12283		Copple R		
26312		Brown W			12378		Copoc H		
12780	L/C	Berry J			13065		Corner E		
14154	Pte	Bateman E.C			12716		Corness H		
25603		Batchelor J			20755		Crank W		
25618		Bradley R			12816		Cobbledick J		
12312		Bushell J			12259		Crosbie J		
12332		Bennett M			12551		Cunningham T		
12358		Brown J			12326		Curran J		
14461		Brown J			12472		Cribley J		
21164		Bridge E.J			25956		Cooper H		
26294		Brooks W			25126		Cathcart W		
12728		Benson J			12248		Coombes A		
18010		Barnes E			14284		Cowen W		
3/11414		Boyle J			25952		Clegg J.B		
12846		Burke J			25958		Cooper W		
13032		Brothwood W			23424		Cairns W		Hospital
12709		Bolden C			12883		Costain E.E	C	
					12809		Code A		
12069	Pte	Chapman J	a		12299		Clegg J.J		
12292	Sgt	Cairns W.H			3/11487		Coombes J		
8989	Pte	Connelly J			13003		Clarkson J		
12045		Cormack W			12959		Clarke C.E		
20734		Crompton J			25696		Clutton E		
20780		Coxhead J			13889		Collister J		
12436		Connor J			13887	Cpl	Crane J		
3/11609		Carter W			25612	Pte	Castell H.J		
13608		Copeland W			25498		Corns C		
12528		Carey J			24118		Cruden J		
13031		Clarke J			25999	Cpl	Crellin W.H		
12961		Crockett E			25917	Pte	Cottrell W		
3/11199		Curry M			25685		Callaghan D		
26434		Connor W			11247		Cubbin J		
12431	Sgt	Campbell D	B		11651		Carley C		
20740	Cpl	Cochran W							

11th (S) Bn. The King's Liverpool Regt. (Pioneers)

No	Rank & Name	Coy	Remarks	No	Rank & Name	Coy	Remarks
8985	Pte Copson C	C		13183	CQMS Day C.P.	C	
26226	" Cragg W	"		18082	Cpl Doyle M	"	
25875	" Coles F.	"		3/11288	Pte Dean J	"	
9536	" Caffrey E	D		12697	" Davies S	"	
26452	" Cowin E	"		20600	" Duffy P	"	
9042	" Calvert J	"		12933	" Dalby M	"	
26450	" Churchill J	"		12914	" Dowling H	"	
10776	" Cookson W	"		12470	" Doran R.	"	
11369	Cpl Chapman J.R.	"		13125	" Downey M	"	
25967	Pte Coope W	"		12422	" Danby J	"	
25622	" Cave A	"		28164	L/C Dixon J.P	"	
12307	" Craven W	"		27944	Pte Dalton J	"	
12793	" Cooper L	"		24400	" Devine W	D	
13809	" Cooper B	"		9013	" Dwyer J	"	
12849	" Cain J	"		26347	" Dale J	"	
12665	" Caton C	"		26248	" Dockerty F.	"	
13131	" Cassidy W	"		26249	" Dockerty R	"	
13903	" Crookes J	"		26330	" Dennis A.E.	"	
20830	" Carr W	"		12490	Sgt Davies S	"	
12932	" Caton J	"		12510	Pte Day A	"	
20426	L/C Cross A.B.	"		21288	" Dickenson W	"	
12937	" Corless J	"		11531	" Dickson H	"	
10593	Cpl Clack J	"		12453	" Dorman W	"	
				13101	" Davies W	"	
23361	Pte Donnegan P	A		20823	" Duffy B	"	
25493	" Deakin A	"		12627	" Dolbel A	"	
21390	" Derrington D	"		18437	Cpl Dodd J	"	
12067	" Dandy J	"		11280	Pte Devereux J	"	
12098	" Devoy E	"					
12109	" Donnelly M	"		8417	Pte Ellis J.	A	
12161	" Davies W.J	"		5980	RSM Edisbury C.H.	"	
21306	" Davies E	"		3/11101	Pte English J	"	
13026	" Davies R	"		12128	" Evans H	"	
21192	" Dyson J	"		18457	" Emslie J	"	
12200	" Dickson J	"		12804	Cpl Evans J	B	
13036	" Devoy J	"		12469	Pte Eaton W	"	
12824	" Dougherty A	"		12206	" Edwards W	"	
10456	" Davies D	"		26617	" Ehrenberg L	"	
18544	" Duffy P	"		12283	" Evans J	"	
11508	" Donaldson J	"		12861	" Evans R	C	
3/11404	" Davies P.	"		21185	" Eccles B	"	
12537	" Derbyshire J	"		14941	L/C Excell J	"	
12077	L/C Dawson S	B		12714	Pte Evans J	"	
21210	Pte Derbyshire J	"		12783	" Edwards N	D	
12302	" Dempsey W	"		~~25205~~	~~#~~		
14448	" Dean J	"	Hospital				
12938	" Dillon J	C		13630	Pte Friedel L	A	
12204	" Duggan C	"		20790	" Fisher J	"	
9887	" Deaken W	"		12153	" Flynn J	"	
25135	" Dickinson P	"		21392	" Holland J	"	
26789	" Dwyer W.H	"					

11th (S) Bn. The King's Liverpool Regt. (Pioneers)

No	Rank	Name	Coy	Remarks	No	Rank	Name	Coy	Remarks
12031	Pte	Fox. J	a		18892	Pte	Gaynor. W	B	
27931	.	Foster J	.		3/11464	RQMS	Gilmore H	C	
26299	.	Fazackley J	.		12755	Sgt	Gillver A	.	
3/11243	.	Fisher W	.		12784	Cpl	Gough J	.	
12231	Sgt	Fardoe H	B		20245	Sgt	Gorst H	.	
13143	Pte	Farrell J	.		12705	L/C	Gordon W	.	
12711	.	Fenton R	.		12703	Pte	Goodwin J	.	
13858	.	Fish J	.		20241	.	Gaskell J	.	
12976	.	Ford C	.		21200	.	Gee J	.	
18245	.	Ford R	.	Checking Xmas Gifts	12910	.	Graham W	.	
					25613	.	Gout R.A.	.	
8678	.	Fletcher J	.		20898	.	Gerrard S	.	
12207	.	Francey H	.		14798	.	Gregory J	.	
12110	.	Fullick A	.		20016	.	Greenfield W	.	
13018	.	Fynberg H	.	Hospital					
12622	Sgt	Franklin W	C		5836	Sgt	Groom G	.	
12818	Pte	Fletcher G	.		25648	Pte	Grundy H.J.	.	
12814	.	Fell G	.		25896	.	Gardner A.F.	D	
18924	.	Fingleton E	.		7066	.	Grady J	.	
26392	.	Fisher H	.		12439	Sgt	Grogan M	.	
28092	.	Frame E	.		25615	Pte	Greaves A.R.	.	
26985	.	Freeman A	.		12715	.	Gaughran J	.	
11546	.	Freeman A	.		18074	.	Griffiths E	.	
27852	.	Ferguson J	.		25617	.	Gilroy J	.	
27139	.	Fitzsimmons J	.		20795	.	Gaffney E	.	
25189	.	Fry J	.		20796	.	Goodbanne G.	.	
20207	.	Flannigan J	D		8011	.	Green W	.	
26301	.	Fenton J	.		8505	.	Goddard E	.	
13038	.	Fazackerly R	.		3/11446	.	Gillespie J	.	
12593	.	Forshaw J	.						
12733	.	Fowler J	.						
26243	.	Fairclough J.E.	.		12025	Pte	Harrison W	a	
					12159	.	Harrison R	.	
23939	Pte	Gledhill G	a		25604	.	Hooper W	.	
10585	Sgt	Gittens P	.		12079	.	Howard D	.	
12913	Pte	Gillow H	.		20602	L/C	Howley A	.	
25986	.	Gale H	.		12037	Cpl	Huyton J	.	
12170	.	Goldsmith R	.		12075	Pte	Hughes W.J.	.	
13120	Sgt	Gane J	.	14th Div H.Qrs.	12097	.	Hughes T	.	
12562	L/C	Gough J.T.	B		12166	.	Hulme W	.	
12240	Pte	Gardner J	.		12168	.	Hetterick P	.	
12663	.	Gee C	.		11413	.	Hoist W	.	
20758	.	Gibbons C	.		21204	.	Hoyes B	.	
12597	.	Gibbons J	.		21252	Cpl	Heaton H.S.	.	
12314	.	Green W	.		12657	Pte	Hayes W	.	
12815	.	Griffiths W	.		21222	.	Hinde J	.	
12652	Pte	Gwilliam T	.		13030	Sgt	Harmon M	B	
11653	.	Garbett C	.		12063	L/C	Haddock W	.	
25121	.	Greenhalgh J	.		13/10236	Pte	Hobbs H	.	
28225	.	Grundy J	.		9044	.	Hassell J	.	
26477	.	Grimes T	.		12408	.	Heald J	.	

11th (S) Bn. The King's Liverpool Regt. (Pioneers)

No	Rank & Name		Coy	Remarks	No	Rank & Name		Coy	Remarks
8984	Pte	Hewitson J	a		12551	Pte	Hope N.V.	D	
8852	.	Howard E	.		13182	.	Hughson J	.	
28260	.	Hyde J	.		12539	.	Hewson J	.	
26335	.	Horne D	.		12973	.	Hall A.H.	.	
20846	.	Hurst A	.		12742	.	Hyslop J	.	
12855	Sgt	Huggins C	B		12980	.	Halton D	.	
9505	.	Hill J	.		11363	.	Harris J	.	
12224	L/C	Herring C	.		11937	.	Hartley J	.	
25146	Pte	Hogarth W	.		26263	.	Haywood H	.	
13876	.	Hilton W	.		27642	L/C	Haines S	.	
12278	.	Hague S	.		27037	Pte	Heath W	.	
20878	.	Halliwell D	.		28261	.	Holding J	.	
13002	.	Havas L	.		25874	.	Hevitty E	.	
13173	.	Hesketh G	.		11075	L/C	Holden J	.	
12670	.	Heywood J	.		12629	Pte	Hines H.P.	.	
12947	.	Higgins C	.		27432	.	Hogan J	.	
23434	.	Hodgson J.H.	.		13707	.	Hogg J	.	
25602	.	Homer J.A.	.		12641	.	Hooligan J	.	
12546	.	Howat J	.		12444	Cpl	Harold J.L.	.	
12581	.	Hoyle J	.		25657	L/S	Hames H	.	
12247	.	Hurst R	.		13736	Pte	Hunt M	.	
12426	.	Hyland J	.		21166	.	Hayes W	.	
27988	.	Hazard R	.		12985	.	Hill J	.	
28610	.	Helliwell W	.		13104	.	Hennesy L	.	
11558	.	Hill W	.		18126	.	Hopkins M	.	
13854	.	Hill J	.		12773	.	Hughes M	.	
8761	.	Harrison E	.						
18253	.	Hennegan J	.						
11352	.	Houghton J	.		26286	Pte	Irvine R.	a	
12807	Cpl	Haskayne A	C		12907	.	Ingram J.H.	D	
12900	Pte	Hewitt J	.		13073	L/C	Irons P	D	
12864	.	Howell R	.						
12800	.	Holt E.G.	.		3/11149	Pte	Jones J	a	
12325	.	Hurst R	.		12504	.	Jackson G	.	
12959	.	Hibbert G.A.	.		12134	.	Johnson J.A.	.	
25626	.	Hawkins A.J.	.		12100	L/C	Jackson J.J.	.	
25616	.	Heron M	.		12073	Pte	Johnson J	.	
12480	.	Hewitt J	.		26132	.	Jones J.H.	.	
12423	.	Hague J	.		25836	.	Jones J	.	
20812	.	Haydock J.J.	.		3/11174	Sgt	Jones H	.	
19417	.	Hargreaves H	.		28150	.	Jarvis R.C.	B	
8727	.	Howarth J	.		12452	Cpl	Jones W	.	
11411	.	Hetherington W	.		12364	Pte	Jackson W	.	
11685	.	Hughes W	.		13920	.	Johnson H	.	Hospital
27436	.	Howarth J	.		12719	.	Johnson W	.	
11492	.	Hewitt W	.		11931	.	Johnson P	.	
13247	.	Hewitt J	.		13558	.	Johnson J	.	
13235	.	Hill J	.		12238	.	Jones J	.	
					21238	.	Jones J	.	

11th (S) Bn. The King's Liverpool Regt. (Pioneers)

No	Rank & Name		Coy	Remarks	No	Rank & Name		Coy	Remarks
12540	Pte	Jones J	B		12277	Pte	Kelly J	D	
7514	.	Jones E	.		12446	.	Kelly J	.	
27143	.	Jones R & W	.		13191	.	Kelly P	.	
12379	.	Johnson H.A.	C		14153	.	Kirk M	.	
12277	.	Johnstone G	.						
21158	.	James R	.		12048	Pte	Lenahen A	a	
20767	.	Jackson J	.		12108	.	Lawson W	.	
12360	.	Jeffers E	.		12934	.	Laird J	.	
12468	.	Johnstone M	.		12040	.	Land J	.	
18789	L/C	Jones W.E.	.		12082	Cpl	Lewis A.S	.	
14744	Pte	Johnson A	.		12874	Pte	Lloyd J	.	
14426	.	Jackson W	.		26256	.	Lewis A	.	
7692	.	Jones W	.		30065	.	Leffler G	.	
26276	.	Jones E	.		12105	.	Loftus W	.	
19908	L/C	Jones E.J	.		3/11772	C.S.M.	Lloyd G.W.	B	
25868	Pte	Jackson W	.		12677	Sgt	Lewis G	.	
30851	.	Jones W.E.	D		12282	Cpl	Lyons M	.	
12547	.	Johnson J	.		12730	.	Lambert T	.	
12754	Cpl	Jones J.H	.	Checking xmas gifts	12233	L/C	Leece W	.	
21123	Pte	Jepson W.A	.		25997	Pte	Lewney J	.	
12802	.	Jones J.J	.		13552	.	Lee J	.	
12575	.	Jaegar W	.		24126	.	Leech J	.	
13070	.	Jennings J	.		12218	.	Linforth G	.	
13162	.	Jaundrell W	.		12347	.	Livingstone R	.	
12535	.	Jennions J	.		13289	.	Lodge H	.	
13116	.	Jelfs W	.		20764	.	Loftus P	.	
12058	Pte	Knight R	a		8429	Sgt	Longshaw J	C	
12092	.	Kirkpatrick A	a		20399	Cpl	Lilliott W	.	
14186	.	Kearney J	.		12865	L/C	Lewis A	.	
3/11241	.	Kenny M	.		12999	Pte	Letcher M	.	
12451	.	Kilbride O	.		12630	.	Little J	.	
21156	.	Kennish J	.		21213	.	Lovatt J	.	
13724	.	Kavanagh R	.		12940	.	Langley J	.	
20517	.	Kershaw J	.		21157	.	Livesey E	.	
12455	.	Kelly M	.		25902	.	Lea A.J	.	
12444	L/C	Kearsley J	B		25846	.	Lewis W.O.	.	
19268	Pte	Kelly J	.		3/11764	Sgt	Lawley A.E.	D	
12521	.	Keogh J	.		26225	Pte	Lomas J	.	
12848	.	Keogh J	.		12418	.	Lawrenson J	.	
12263	.	King A	.		13135	.	Lumbeck A	.	
~~	.	R	.		13151	.	Lathe J	.	
12339	.	Kelly J	C		12435	.	Lewis J	.	
13015	.	Kitt A	.						
12650	.	Kaye S	.						
12633	.	Kennedy J	.		28175	Pte	Muldoon J	a	
20745	Pte	Kennish J.J.	.		12015	.	Murphy J	.	
10667	.	Kayes D	.		25955	.	Murdoch J	.	
25861	.	Kewley J	.		12022	.	Madigan R	.	
25129	.	Kearsley J	.		12700	.	Murray A	.	
					12111	.	Murray J	.	

11th (S) Bn. The King's Liverpool Regt. (Pioneers)

No	Rank	Name	Coy		No	Rank	Name	Coy	Remarks
12060	Pte	Maver W	A		7397	Pte	Mudie H	B	
12946	"	McGarry H	"		10537	"	Millbanks M	"	
12061	"	McCabe E	"		11014	"	McArdle M	"	
12124	"	McNulty R	"		11948	"	Morgan D	"	
21215	"	Morgan W	"		26261	"	Money JW	"	
12320	"	Meadows C	"		26948	"	Mason J	"	
20700	"	Morris H	"		12556	Sgt	MacDonald D	C	Checking Xmas gifts
12143	"	Mills R	"		12936	"	Moss WS	"	
12834	"	Moorhead D	"		12344	Cpl	Minards J	"	
12164	L/C	Moore W	"		12383	"	Mitchell J	"	
12183	Pte	Moran J	"		12361	Pte	Melia J	"	
12186	"	Meleady J	"		13045	"	Magill J	"	
12402	"	Maloney J	"		24142	"	Morley J	"	
12192	"	Mousley J	"		12771	"	Melville J	"	
12033	"	Maines H	"		12586	"	Martin S	"	
12199	"	Mullaly M	"		20760	"	Maloney P	"	
8044	"	Moran J	"		21393	"	Mellhuish HJ	"	
12062	"	Masterson J	"		21216	"	Mullinger J	"	
12236	L/C	Murphy B	"		12474	"	Melia J	"	
9444	CSM	Mitchell J	"		12471	"	Morgan J	"	
26973	Pte	Mills A	"		12483	"	Murray J	"	
20735	"	Mather A	"		12455	"	Mahoney H	"	
25936	"	Murphy H	"		13544	"	Martin W	"	
25259	"	Mousley W	"		13489	"	Murphy J	"	
25992	"	Masheter J	"		12403	"	Morrison W	"	
12074	"	McBride M	"		11044	"	Masterson M	"	
14147	"	McFadden J	"	Road Controls	26206	"	Mort J	"	
12346	Cpl	Marchbank J	B		28274	"	Meehan J	"	
12205	"	Munroe J	"		25891	"	McDermott S	"	
10692	L/C	Marsh H	"		12542	L/C	Megann J	D	
12357	"	Murphy E	"		11170	Pte	Martin S	"	
12443	Pte	McEvoy P	"		25963	"	Mitchell W	"	
12245	"	McGarry J	"		26236	"	Marshall W	"	
13362	"	McGregor J	"		3/11035	Sgt	McKinney A	"	
12888	"	McGuinness E	"		3/12034	"	Murray J	"	
13908	"	McIntyre J	"		27049	Pte	Murdoch E	"	
20758	"	McKenzie J	"		20828	"	Moss SJ	"	
12374	"	McQuiggan J	"		13021	"	Mason W	"	
12487	"	Muller J	"		12514	"	Marsden J	"	
21244	"	Millington A	"		12767	"	McKnight J	"	
12813	"	Molloy E	"		12563	"	McKee W	"	
12300	"	Morgan J	"		12478	"	McCrann D	"	
23796	"	Morris M	"		12740	"	McVey J	"	
21205	"	Moss J	"		12454	"	McKenna J	"	
12261	"	Murchie A	"		12414	"	McIntyre P	"	
12250	"	Murdoch J	"		13171	"	McQuillam J	"	
12309	"	Murphy J	"		12286	"	Moran W	"	
12438	"	Murray A	"		12982	"	Moore J	"	
20782	"	Myler R	"		21150	"	May J	"	
13124	"	McKenzie J	"		13270	"	Murphy J	"	

11th (S) Bn. The King's Liverpool Regt. (Pioneers)

No	Rank & Name		Coy	Remarks	No	Rank & Name		Coy	Remarks
21219	Pte	Mitchell E.	D		12193	Pte	Pitt A	a	
13193		Mulligan J			12198		Penny H		
7674		McLennon A			12542		Pickford W		
12197		McHenry J			12052		Plaice F		
					12007	Sgt	Pugh H		
					3/12111	Pte	Packham R		
27161	Pte	Naylor H	B		27164	Cpl	Pitt J.C.		
12687		Nolan J			28170	Pte	Parker J		
12820		Nolan M			9505		Parker P		
13100		Nulty J			9856	CQMS	Payne J	B	
12270		Nicholson R.J.	C		10552	Cpl	Paterson		
19902		Nuttall H			11069	Pte	Price W		
12464		Nelder W			25497		Parker R		
18931		Nixon G.E.			12744		Parker W		
12997		Newman S			20807		Pickup F		
8869		Naylor H			13761		Porter P		
14293		Newsham J			20849		Proctor R		
3/11096	Sgt	Neal W	D		12863		Parker J		
26237	Pte	Napper J			3/11463	CSM	Powell H	C	
12872	Cpl	Newall F.C.			12896	Pte	Platt R		
11250	Pte	Newman S			12854		Pullinhorn H		
12876		Nuttall J			12760		Pugh W		
12538		Nield J			12747		Partridge G		
					12557		Patten G		
12078	Pte	Owens D	a		21131		Power W.W.A.		
12526		O'Connell J			18938		Phillips G.H.		
3/11367	Cpl	O'Brien P			9036		Partington R		
13674	Pte	O'Neill P			25156		Perry J		
25844		O'Mara J			12904		Payne E		
27266		O'Prey E			25899		Pierce G	D	
11579	L/C	O'Brien A	B		12723	Cpl	Partridge S		
12293	Pte	O'Brien J			12142	Sgt	Preston A.W.		
12169		Ormisher E			12838	Pte	Peters G		
12280		Ockleshaw J			12242		Pierce W.H.		
20842		O'Neill J			12961		Potter R		
21163		Ogden J.C.	C		25610		Phillips S.R.		
14496	L/C	Owen H			12654		Price P		
19891	Pte	Oakley J.W.			12790		Price H		
11989	L/C	Orton W			25623		Prior H		
3/10640		Owen L.D.	D		12945		Pugh W		
23155		Oppery J.E.			13132		Purslow A		
					25619		Pringle A		
					26351		Pettit J.W.		
25495	Pte	Power J.W.	a						
12036		Pulford H	-		12512	L/C	Quigley J	a	
12043	L/C	Parry A		Road Controls	13186	Pte	Quayle A.S.	C	
12968	Cpl	Parry W			12192		Quayle J	D	
12407	Pte	Parry J							
12165		Pye J							

11th (S) Bn. The King's Liverpool Regt. (Pioneers)

No	Rank	Name	Coy	Remarks	No	Rank	Name	Coy	Remarks
9064	Sgt	Rawson T.J.	A		12482	Pte	Roberts J.	D	
10647	Pte	Rock J.			12286	.	Robinson J.	.	
3/11104	.	Rohenbeck J.	.		13096	.	Robinson T.M.	.	
25492	.	Rawson J.	.		12853	.	Rigby J.	.	
12895	.	Rimmer T.	.		13187	.	Rowlands J.	.	
12021	.	Rimmer J.	.		21257	.	Rawson J.	.	
12041	.	Ready J.	.		12707	.	Richards J.	.	
20762	.	Robinson H.	.		12503	.	Roscoe W.	.	
21253	.	Rigby T.	.						
12972	.	Roberts W.	.		12014	Pte	Saunders W.	A	
13188	.	Redpath J.	.		20818	.	Sykes R.	.	
12576	.	Rogers J.	.		20804	.	Selby S.	.	
8439	.	Riding J.	.		12806	.	Shelford R.	.	
18649	.	Robinson J.	.		20686	.	Seothern J.	.	
13452	.	Roberts J.	.		20822	.	Scott A.	.	
27641	.	Reece W.	.		12407	.	Shakespeare J.	.	
3/11884	Sgt	Rawlings W.	B		21307	.	Smalley A.	.	
13537	L/C	Reardon E.	.		3/12169	.	Stewart A.	.	
9203	Pte	Robinson A.	.		12981	.	Simpkins J.	.	
7003	.	Roberts W.	.		12984	.	Simpkins J.	.	
12481	.	Rice P.	.		20752	L/C	Smith J.	.	
12268	.	Rimmer B.	.		12035	Cpl	Sudbury R.	.	
13612	.	Roberts C.	.		12026	Pte	Staunton J.	.	
12235	.	Robinson W.	.		19256	Sgt	Spilling C.	.	
12350	.	Rowland J.	.		28211	Pte	Smith T.	.	Hospital
12795	.	Rowley W.	.		12308	.	Spencer J.	.	
26210	.	Reynolds A.	C		12189	.	Stokes J.	.	
12363	.	Ridyard W.	.		13164	Cpl	Smith J.	B	
13029	.	Roberts A.	.		27157	Pte	Sunderland W.	.	
18403	.	Rimmer J.	.		9039	.	Solden S.	.	
12572	.	Rooney J.	.		25962	.	Sutton C.	.	
25928	.	Raey D.L.	.		9261	.	Southall W.	.	
25890	.	Teaney M.	.		12623	.	Sargeant H.	.	
12391	.	Ryan J.	.		12963	.	Silverman J.	.	
25162	.	Ryder J.	.		12990	.	Simlo R.	.	
12821	Sgt	Robinson R.	D		12243	.	Simms W.	.	
8056	L/C	Roberts J.	.	P.O. Hazebruk	12290	.	Simpson J.	.	
12851	Pte	Ramsey J.	.		24009	.	Slimm H.W.	.	
25891	.	Ranger T.	.		25964	.	Stott W.	.	
12403	L/C	Roberts J.	.		13165	.	Smith E.	.	
21296	Pte	Ritchie G.	.		25606	.	Smith E.	.	
12311	.	Reay J.	.		12269	.	Stoba E.	.	
13092	.	Reveille E.	.		12765	Cpl	Smart D.	C	
12462	.	Reynolds B.	.		12805	Pte	Smith G.H.	.	
12631	.	Richardson J.	.		12385	L/C	Shelbourne A.	.	
12734	.	Rick J.	.		12380	Pte	Spencer L.	.	
13297	.	Ripley P.	.						
12508	.	Roberts D.	.						

11th (S) Bn. The King's Liverpool Regt. (Pioneers)

No	Rank	Name	Coy	Remarks	No	Rank	Name	Coy	Remarks
12323	Pte	Smith J	C		10921	Pte	Taylor H R	a	
13022	.	Smith A	.		3/13572	Cpl	Taylor K.J.	.	
12991	.	Stott C	.		12018	Pte	Thomas J	.	
20456	.	Stamp W	.		20832	.	Timmins J	.	
21292	.	Eungleton W	.		12055	.	Turner J a	.	
21214	.	Shore S	.		12178	.	Travers S	.	
18835	.	Smith E	.		12006	.	Teasdale J	.	
12926	.	Stafford J	.		12104	.	Taylor R	.	
25614	.	Stanton G A	.		13812	.	Thornton J	.	
19953	.	Simpson C E	.		10718	.	Thompson J	.	
19939	.	Smith A.E.	.		3/11309	.	Traynor J	.	
26464	.	Stubbert J	.		12486	.	Taylor J	B	
11226	.	Smith J W	.		12234	.	Taylor J	.	
14323	Cpl	Spruce J.G.	.		21160	.	Taylor J a	.	
8911	Pte	Sherry J	.		25525	.	Tyrer C	.	
10610	.	Scott J	.		26253	.	Taggart H	.	
13690	.	Shaw E	.		12274	Sgt	Thomas J J	C	
10821	.	Sandon J	.		12956	L/C	Tait D	.	
11605	.	Seddon J	.		19982	Pte	Thompson E	.	
26447	.	Sutton J	D		12737	.	Totten R	.	
26363	.	Standish J	.		12498	.	Traynor J P	.	
13269	.	Shelbourne A	.		20854	.	Tennant W	.	
25996	.	Sutcliffe L	.		21179	.	Tatham a	.	
12583	.	Sharples B	.		14485	.	Tysoe G T	.	
7346	CQMS	Salisbury J.E.	.		28047	.	Thornley a	.	
9186	CSM	Smith C	.		48896	.	Tartt J J	.	
20829	L/C	Sumner E	.		13682	.	Traynor J	.	
12343	Cpl	Smith W	.		3/12386	Sgt	Taylor W	D	
21304	Pte	Saunders H	.		11287	Pte	Talbot J	.	
21293	.	Stabler J	.	Hospital	26258	.	Townsend R	.	
12310	.	Sedgewick A	.		12621	.	Taylor H	.	
13102	.	Shingler G	.		20707	.	Thirton G T	.	
20442	.	Simpson H	.		12492	.	Turner J	.	
12996	.	Smithurst P	.		20775	.	Tinsley J	.	
12463	L/C	Snowden G	.		12386	.	Teveney W	.	
3/11158	Pte	Steging G6	.		30504	Cpl	Trigg W	B	
12549	.	Squire E	.		12569	Pte	Vinne S	D	
26446	.	Salt H	.		25991	.	Vickers W	.	
9403	.	Smallman J	.		3/12508	CQMS	Wright E	a	
12513	.	Sowbutts G	.		13093	Cpl	White a	.	
					12675	Pte	Warburton J	.	
					12008	.	Williams a	.	
12252	Sgt	Tipton J	a		12158	.	Wilson T	.	
12010	Cpl	Toole E	.		12096	.	Williams S	.	
25600	Pte	Talbot H	.		12056	L/C	Woods S	.	
12048	.	Taylor S	.		12087	Pte	Whittaker H	.	

11th (S) Bn. The King's Liverpool Regt. (Pioneers)

No	Rank	Name	Coy	Remarks	No	Rank	Name	Coy	Remarks
12441	L/C	Waller T	A		27252	Pte	White B	B	
12109	Pte	Worrall S	.		13097	L/S	Woods G	D	
14170	.	Whittingham J	.		12626	Cpl	Woods W	.	
28168	.	Whitehead J	.		20779	.	White E	.	
13433	.	Williams W	.		12903	Pte	Wilson W	.	
9268	.	Walker G	.		23307	.	Woods R	.	
20502	Sgt	Walker E	.		12667	.	Wallis J	.	
13158	.	Wilson R	B		25923	.	Wilson T	.	
12284	L/S	Willis W	.		19421	.	Wray J	.	
20821	Pte	Walker J	.		21130	.	Wade J	.	
20877	.	Walker L	.	Hospital	12684	.	Whitelaw W	.	
12558	.	Warburton J	.		12763	.	Williams J	.	
12355	.	Williams A	.		12853	.	Winders A	.	
14152	.	Wilson J	.		20783	L/C	Woods T J	.	
20798	.	Wilmore T	.		3/11770	Pte	Woods J	.	
20835	.	Winterbottom H	.		13046	.	Woodcock J	.	
24120	.	Woodward R	.		21161	.	Walmsley J	.	
12817	.	Wright T	.		26338	.	Williams C	.	
12365	.	Wright J	.		25938	.	Welsh S	.	
8328	.	Wylie L	.	at Base for Discharge	13804	.	Williams J	.	
25706	.	Watkinson P	.		13077	.	Wheeler G	.	
27750	.	Walsh D	.						
25834	.	Ward JH	.						
9662	.	Williams H	.						
18272	Cpl	Why A	C						
12389	Pte	Wroe T	.						
12381	.	Ward J	.		21249	Pte	Yates Y	B	
12342	.	Wilson J	.		12122	.	Yeo H	C	
13095	.	White J	.		12795	.	Yates T	D	
3/10834	.	Willox W	.		12943	.	Youdes H	D	
12692	.	Williams J	.						
12664	.	Williams J	.		**Attached**				
12655	.	Walsh P	.		1449	Arm Sgt Sgt	Nunn T W	B	
12648	.	Woods AH	.						
12584	.	Wright J	.						
20841	.	Woods H	.						
25621	.	Whitehead HW	.	Hospital					
12432	.	Williams W	.						
25887	.	Welsh J	.						
26271	.	Webb J	.						
13616	.	Woods W	.						
11919	.	Whittaker J	.	Road Control					
28214	.	Warden J	.						
11230	.	White J	.						
11469	L/C	Woods A	.						
7507	.	Waft R	.						
21270	.	Worthington W	.						

Roll of Officers — 11th (S) Bn. The King's Liverpool Regt. (Pioneers)

Rank	Name	Remarks
Major	E. C. Ogle	Command
Captain	G. S. Mitchell	
"	H. Johnson	
" & Adjt	G.E.A. Browne	
"	A.F. Trotter	
"	F. E. Long	
"	H. Paget	
Lieutenant	M.C.M. Denny	
"	A. Chavasse	
"	H.R. Bennett	
"	J.S. Goodacre	
"	R. Knox Paton	O.C Reinforcements, Base
"	D. Stanton	
"	G. J. Harris	
2nd Lieutenant	W.R.A. Wareing	
"	H. Brereton	
"	G.H. Hopkins	
"	H. Kent	
"	E.L. Austen	
"	H.A. Fox	
"	P.H.G. Pye-Smith	
"	H.M. Beckwith-Towse	
"	J.P.C. Sorge	
"	R.G. Chadwick	
"	S. Geake	
Lieutenant	H.W. Taylor	R.A.M.C
Lieut-Col	V.J. Bailey	Wounded in Hospital, England
Lieut & QM	H. Callaghan	do do do

E.C. Ogle Major Commdg.
11th (S) Bn. The King's Liverpool Regt. (Pioneers)

7.Y.
(5 sheets)

11th L:pool
Vol: 7

R/14

14

Pioneers

Confidential

War diary of
11th (S) Bn. The King's Liverpool Regt. (Pioneers)

From 1st January 1916.   To 31st
                          January 1916

(Volume. VII).

WAR DIARY or INTELLIGENCE SUMMARY.

Army Form C. 2118.

(Erase heading not required.)

Instructions regarding War Diaries and Intelligence Summaries are contained in F.S. Regs., Part II. and the Staff Manual respectively. Title pages will be prepared in manuscript.

Place	Date	Hour	Summary of Events and Information	Remarks and references to Appendices
ELVERDINGHE	Jan 2		Regiment by different trench streamers. 3 Companies working on trenches; one on trolley line and Camp. 1 Casualty wounded by shrapnel about to be partly decorated; one notified M.C.O., O.H. died	HP
"	Jan 3		3 companies on trenches; one in Camp & on trolley line; 3 casualties wounded by shrapnel	HP
"	Jan 4		3 companies on trenches A for 42nd Bde; B for 41st Bde; D for 43rd Bde; one Company on Divl. Signals and tramways; 2	HP
"	Jan 5		3 companies on trenches; 1 Company on Signals. Slight shelling of ELVERDINGHE. 1 Casualty wounded by shrapnel	See
"	Jan 6		3 companies on trenches; one Coy on tramway & Signals. 1 Casualty wounded by shrapnel	See
"	Jan 7		3 companies on trenches; one Coy on Tramway & Signals.	See
"	Jan 8		3 Coys at work in trenches; one Coy on Tramway and signals. No casualties.	See
"	Jan 9		As above. 3 men killed, Eight men wounded in trenches.	See
"	Jan 10th–11th		As above. No casualties	See
"	12th		As above. No casualties.	See
"	13th		As above. by Casualties.	See
"	14th		As above. One casualty one killed one wounded.	R.C.O
"	15th		As above. Casualties 2 O.R. killed & one wounded.	S. Lay
"	16th		As above. No casualties 2 NCOs wounded some man	Eff.
"	17th		As above. No casualties	Eff.
"	Jan 18		As above. No casualties.	Eff.
"	Jan 19		As above. One casualty wounded.	Eff.
"	Jan 20		As above. No casualties	Eff.
"	Jan 21		As above. One casualty wounded	Eff.

Army Form C. 2118.

WAR DIARY
or
INTELLIGENCE SUMMARY.
(Erase heading not required.)

Instructions regarding War Diaries and Intelligence Summaries are contained in F. S. Regs., Part II. and the Staff Manual respectively. Title pages will be prepared in manuscript.

Place	Date	Hour	Summary of Events and Information	Remarks and references to Appendices
ELVERDINGHE	Jan 22		Continuing on trenches and tramways	
"	" 23		Do above. One casualty wounded	
"	" 24		As above. No casualties	
"	" 25		Do above. One casualty wounded	
"	" 26		Do above. No casualties	
"	" 27		Do above. Casualties one man killed & one man gun shunned	
"	" 28		Do above. Casualties from wounds, 3 only slightly	
"	" 29		As above. No casualties	
"	" 30		As above. One casualty wounded. R/C Lt Col P Churchie joined for duty	
"	" 31		As above. One casualty wounded	
"	Feb 1		As above. Strength 4 Offrs of H & Barhams, 20 to & Surver attached for instruction. No Casualties	

8.Y.
(8 sheets)

11th Kings
Liverpool
Vol. 8.
H, J & K

Confidential

War Diary
of

11th (S) Bn. The King's Liverpool Regt. (Pioneers)

From 1st February, 1916 To 29th February, 1916

(Volume VIII)

[signature] Capt & ?/Lt.-Colonel,
Commdg. 11th (S) Bn. King's L'pool Regt. (Pioneers)

WAR DIARY

INTELLIGENCE SUMMARY.

(Erase heading not required.)

Army Form C. 2118.

Place	Date	Hour	Summary of Events and Information	Remarks and references to Appendices
ENVERDINGHE		1st Wk	Three companies worked on two obstacles one company on tripods & tripwire & tripwire. & Officers & NCOs of Murrihead Johnson Shillito instructed 16 canals to this company worked on trenches one company on tripods & tramways.	Appx
"		2nd "	ditto above	Appx
"		3rd "	" "	Appx
"		4th "	As above. One casualty wounded	Appx
"		5th "	" " No casualties	Appx
"		6th "	" " As above. One man wounded	Appx
"		7th "	As above. One man wounded	Appx
"		8th "	As above. No casualties	Appx
"		9th "	As above. No casualties	Appx
"		10th "	As above. One casualty wounded	
Abb. Sheet 23 "Hot Camp"		11th "	Two Companies proceeded to Hol Camp prior to relief 2 Co M.Graham & Capt S Brigham & Ayremas	Appx
"		12th	Two Companies on the Canal Bank were relieved by two Coys of 11th R. A 16. A sheet 27. The calculated occurs Ambush threatened at Hol Camp. A 16. A sheet 27. He made 2 H Brown The transport was split up into two parties one relieved & the other 2nd S.Welch Coys no longer required but remained to us to the two Welch coys or change at Ellercamp at 5 pm. Orders were received at 5 p.m. then confirmed by W/m & lines put by W/m allows fresh to that part of the Transport with 21st E. Coy to move off at 9.20 am.	Appx
LEDRINGHEM	13		that part of the Transport with 21st E. Coy to move off at 9.15 am. Unit can escort B 2o Coy from B/Cry to LEDRINGHEM in 10 or lorry HD or lorry LEDRINGHEM & Battalion was conveyed by HD or lorry to their billets we have occupied since we have been in France where they took up their billets. Since we have been in this area the Battalion spent today in cleaning up from their long journey & taking necessary precaution against fire.	Appx

Army Form C. 2118.

WAR DIARY
~~INTELLIGENCE~~ SUMMARY.
(Erase heading not required.)

Instructions regarding War Diaries and Intelligence Summaries are contained in F.S. Regs., Part II. and the Staff Manual respectively. Title pages will be prepared in manuscript.

Place	Date	Hour	Summary of Events and Information	Remarks and references to Appendices
	Jul			
LEDRINGHEM	15th	7.15am	Physical Drill	
		9-12.30p	Section, Platoon & Company drill & Machine Gun & Bombing instruction	
		2-3p	Extended Order Drill Instruction see 4th & 5th instructions would impart as on 16th	Ikel
LEDRINGHEM	16th	7.7.30	Drill Order Inspection by OC Companies	
		10am	Attendrill in for 400 instruction	
		10.5am	Message rec of that 800 14 Wounded applied hot inspect in carrying of the appts. available	
		10 45tn	Lecture by Company Officers	tho
		12-1pm	Lecture by CO to all Officers	
		2.3p	Extended order Drill & Machine Gun instruction & Bombing carried out	
EDRINGHEM	17th	7-7.30	Physical Drill 2nd Inspection & 5 other ranks proceeded to KAENEKE Kentain for antiair instruction as arranged billeting party	
do	do	9-13.0p	Route March	DRS
		2.30.3	Foot inspection	
do do	18th	7.7.30	Physical Drill	
		9.12.30p	Lecture, on account of bad weather no drill was possible	
		2.3p	Battalion prepared for move on 19th inst-	DRS

WAR DIARY
INTELLIGENCE SUMMARY.
(Erase heading not required.)

Army Form C. 2118.

Place	Date	Hour	Summary of Events and Information	Remarks and references to Appendices
	Feb			
LEDRINGHEM	19th	6 a.m.	Reveille packed kitbags for store	
		8 a.m.	Three motor lorries arrived for Huts & baggage & moved to CASSEL station	
		9.45	Horse transport and A Company moved off to CASSEL	
		12.45p	B & D Companies moved off to CASSEL	
CASSEL		4 p.m.	A B D Companies and 2/3 transport left CASSEL by train for unknown destination	
LONGUEAU	20th	8 am	arrived LONGUEAU & detrained	
LEDRINGHEM	19th	1.45p	C Company & remainder of transport left for CASSEL	
CASSEL		6 p.m.	C Company & remainder of transport left CASSEL	
LONGUEAU	20th	6 a.m.	do arrived LONGUEAU	
"		5 a.m.	A, C, B, D & HQrs & Coy Longueau for VILLERS BOCAGE arriving at 9 am by two routes	
"		8 am	C Company do do do - took the do	
VILLERS BOCAGE		12 noo	Transport arrived. Getted billets	Wind
"	21st	7.7½	Physical drill	
		9.12	Shell, Section, Platoon & Company	
		2-3	Company drill	Grass

Army Form C. 2118.

WAR DIARY
or
~~INTELLIGENCE~~ SUMMARY.
(Erase heading not required.)

Instructions regarding War Diaries and Intelligence Summaries are contained in F.S. Regs., Part II. and the Staff Manual respectively. Title pages will be prepared in manuscript.

Place	Date	Hour	Summary of Events and Information	Remarks and references to Appendices
Villers BOCAGE	Feb 22nd	4-7.30	Physical drill	
		9.11.30	Route March	
		2-3	Company drill Machine Gun & Lewis gun instruction, Musketry, transport	Ahd
do	do 23rd	7.7.30	Physical drill	
		9.11.30	Company, platoon section drill extended order drill Machine Gun & Bombing Instruction	
		2-3	Extended order drill	HCS
do do		11am	Orders received Re a readiness move at short notice	
do do	24th	8am	Orders received Move at 10.30 am Billets/pass turned off	HCS
do do		10am	Battalion fell in & half transport	
		11am	Remainder of Transport moved off	
AUTHIEULE		3pm	Battalion arrived AUTHIEULE and billetted for the night	HCS
"	25th	8am	Orders received to move to WARLURZEL	
		10am	Battalion marched out in a snowstorm	
		4.30p	Battalion arrived less transport except cookers & pedlar horses for transport	
		11.30	Horse transport arrived & Battalion remainder & Cookers turned up	HCS

Army Form C. 2118.

WAR DIARY
or
INTELLIGENCE SUMMARY.
(Erase heading not required.)

Place	Date	Hour	Summary of Events and Information	Remarks and references to Appendices
WARLUZEL	Feb 26	12 noon	Remainder of transport arrived priest another platoon.	etc
"	27	11 am	Church parade	1 Sheet
"	28th	1 am	Orders were received to move at 10am to FOSSEUX	
"		7 am	Billeting party moved off	
"		10 am	Battalion & transport moved off	
FOSSEUX		12.30pm	Battalion arrived & moved into Billets	ESAS
"			In the afternoon Billets were cleaned & put into order.	
"	29th	9-12	Company, platoon, section & extended order drill	ENS
"		2-3	Lectures	

WAR DIARY
~~INTELLIGENCE~~ SUMMARY.
(Erase heading not required.)

Army Form C. 2118.

Instructions regarding War Diaries and Intelligence Summaries are contained in F. S. Regs., Part II. and the Staff Manual respectively. Title pages will be prepared in manuscript.

Place	Date	Hour	Summary of Events and Information	Remarks and references to Appendices
FOSSEUX	March 1st	9-12	Company, platoon, section & extended order drill	Nil.
"	March 2nd	2-3p	As above	Nil.
"	"	" 2-3p	Smoke helmet drill	
"	March 3rd		Company, platoon, smoke helmet drill	
"	"	2-3p	Lectures	
"	"		Orders were received that Battalion would move on the 4th inst. Half the Battalion	Nil.
"	"		to ARRAS and the remainder to DAINVILLE.	
"	4th	Midday	Transport was packed prior to move	
"	"	2p	Transport moved off in snow storm	
"	"	4p	Battalion moved off. A & B companies to ARRAS, C by L ACHICOURT and	Nil.
"	"		C. Workshops & Transport & HQ to DAINVILLE	
DAINVILLE	" 5th	8pm	C by Workshops & Transport arrived. A & B Coys bivouc ARRAS and D.C. at ACHICOURT	Nil.
"	"		General settling down in new Billets	
"	"		All Companies reconnoitred the trenches	Nil.
"	"		2nd Lt E. McGlade joined for duty	

WAR DIARY
or
INTELLIGENCE SUMMARY.
(Erase heading not required.)

Army Form C. 2118.

Place	Date	Hour	Summary of Events and Information	Remarks and references to Appendices
DRANOUTRE	6th		A.B.D Companies commenced work on communication trenches. "C"Company two platoons on trenches one platoon working on signal lines one platoon on R.E fatigues. Workshops were reformed. No casualties.	(1)
"	7th		A.B.D Companies continued work on communication trenches. "C"Company two platoons on trenches one platoon working on signal lines one platoon on R.E fatigues. No casualties.	(2)
"	8th		A.B.D Companies continued work on communication trenches. "C"Company two platoons on trenches one platoon working on signal lines on platoon on R.E fatigues. No casualties.	(3)
"	9th		A.B.D Companies continued work on communication trenches. "C"Company two platoons on trenches one platoon working on signal lines one platoon on R.E fatigues. No casualties.	(4)
"	10th		A.B.D Companies continued work on communication trenches. "C"Company three platoons on trenches, one platoon rested on signal lines one platoon on R.E fatigues. No casualties. 2nd Lt H.G Thomas & Hallam joined for duty.	(5)

Army Form C. 2118.

WAR DIARY
or
INTELLIGENCE SUMMARY.
(Erase heading not required.)

Instructions regarding War Diaries and Intelligence Summaries are contained in F.S. Regs., Part II. and the Staff Manual respectively. Title pages will be prepared in manuscript.

Place	Date	Hour	Summary of Events and Information	Remarks and references to Appendices
DAINVILLE	March 11th		A.B.D. Companies continued work on communication trenches.	M.S.
ARRAS	12th		"C" Company moved to ARRAS. The Companies Headquarters & A.B.C. Companies are now in ARRAS. D Company at ACHICOURT. Companies continued repair work on trenches. There were no casualties.	M.S.
ARRAS	13th		A.B.D. Companies continued work on communication trenches. C Company laid a cable line for the signals. There were no casualties.	E.W.
"	14th		as above	E.W.
"	15th		A.B.D. Companies continued work on communication trenches. C Company had no platoon working for signals C party on burying dugouts of the commander in chief Reference of ARRAS. There were no casualties.	E.W.
"	16th		as above	E.W.
"	17		as above. One casualty slightly wounded.	M.S.
"	18th		A.B.D. Companies continued work on communication trenches. C Company had one platoon working for signals, one platoon on dugouts to commander in chief & A. still formed K duty.	M.S.

Army Form C. 2118.

WAR DIARY
or
INTELLIGENCE SUMMARY.
(Erase heading not required.)

Instructions regarding War Diaries and Intelligence Summaries are contained in F.S. Regs., Part II. and the Staff Manual respectively. Title pages will be prepared in manuscript.

Place	Date	Hour	Summary of Events and Information	Remarks and references to Appendices
ARRAS	Oct 19th		A.B.D Companies continued work on communication trenches. C Company had one platoon working for engineers, one platoon on dugout construction, from emplacements to trenches in ARRAS defences. Casualties. One wounded.	Ques.
"	20th		As above. Casualties. Two wounded	ques.
"	21st		as above. No casualties.	ques.
"	22nd		As above. No casualties.	ques.
"	23rd		as above. No casualties.	ques.
"	24th		as above. No casualties.	ques.
"	25th		as above. No casualties.	ques.
"	26th		as above. No casualties.	ques.
"	27th		as above. No casualties.	ques.
"	28.		as above. A March carpenter Coy was fired on Arras on this date. No casualties.	ques.
"	29		A.B.D Companies continued work on communication trenches. C Company commenced work with whole company on Arras defences only. 4 experienced Signallers were lent to the Divisional Signal Company	ques.

Army Form C. 2118.

WAR DIARY
or
INTELLIGENCE SUMMARY.

(Erase heading not required.)

Instructions regarding War Diaries and Intelligence Summaries are contained in F. S. Regs., Part II. and the Staff Manual respectively. Title pages will be prepared in manuscript.

Place	Date	Hour	Summary of Events and Information	Remarks and references to Appendices
ARRAS	July 30.		A, B & C Companies continued work on communication trench. "C" Company worked on Arras defences & Machine Gun Emplacements. Mined dugouts. The usual party employed with Divisional Signal Coy. There were no casualties.	Strength Return.
	31st		As above	As above.

~~XXV~~ ~~Confidential~~ Vol X

War Diary
of.
11th. (S) Bn. Kings Liverpool Regiment
(Pioneers).

~~From~~ 1st April 1916
To.   30th April 1916

(Volume X)

10-Y.
(A Wheeler)

Army Form C. 2118.

WAR DIARY
INTELLIGENCE SUMMARY.
(Erase heading not required.)

Instructions regarding War Diaries and Intelligence Summaries are contained in F. S. Regs., Part II. and the Staff Manual respectively. Title pages will be prepared in manuscript.

Place	Date	Hour	Summary of Events and Information	Remarks and references to Appendices
ARRAS	Apl 1.		A.B.D. Companies continued work on communication trenches. "C" Company worked on Arras defences & supplied 3 teams of miners for dugouts. Five NCOs & men were attached to 184 Tunnel Coy^d Company for dangerous work. Strength of Coy by return there were no casualties.	
"	2nd		As above	Nil
"	3rd		As above	Nil
"	4th		As above	As above no casualties	Nil
"	5th		As above	As above no casualties	Nil
"	6th		As above	As above Cowell & Clift wounded. Clift	Nil
"	7th		As above	As above successfully wounded	Nil
"	8th		As above	As above no casualties	Nil
"	9th		As above	As above two men died from natural causes	Nil
"	10th		As above	As above no casualties	Nil
"	11th		As above	As above no casualties	Nil
"	12th		As above	As above no casualties	Nil

Army Form C. 2118.

WAR DIARY
INTELLIGENCE SUMMARY.
(Erase heading not required.)

Instructions regarding War Diaries and Intelligence Summaries are contained in F. S. Regs., Part II. and the Staff Manual respectively. Title pages will be prepared in manuscript.

Place	Date	Hour	Summary of Events and Information	Remarks and references to Appendices
ARRAS	April 13.		No. 1 Company continued work on communication trenches. "C" Company worked on Arras defences & supplied 3 teams of drivers for dugouts. Five Motormen worked with Lt Steveson Signal Company. There were no casualties.	
"	14th		As above. There were no casualties.	Clear
"	15th		As above. There were no casualties	Clear
"	16th		As above. There were no casualties	Clear
"	17th		As above	Clear
"	18th		As above	Clear
"	19th		As above	Clear
"	20th		As above	Clear
"	21st		As above. One casualty. Number two casualty received 2nd Lt G Smith	
"	22nd		No other news. C/152 Company continued work on communication trench. "C" Company worked on Area defence. Supplied 3 teams of drivers for dugouts. Five Motormen worked for Lt Steveson Signal Company. There were no casualties	Clear
"	23.		As above. No above there were no casualties	Clear

WAR DIARY

INTELLIGENCE SUMMARY

Army Form C. 2118.

(Erase heading not required.)

Instructions regarding War Diaries and Intelligence Summaries are contained in F.S. Regs., Part II. and the Staff Manual respectively. Title pages will be prepared in manuscript.

Place	Date	Hour	Summary of Events and Information	Remarks and references to Appendices
Arras	Apl 24th		A.B.D Companies continued work on communication trenches. "C" Company worked on Arras defences & supplied 3 teams of miners for dugouts. Two Notesmen worked for 1st Division Signal Company. There were no casualties. The Army Commander, General Sir Edmund Allenby sent down to the A.R.R.S defences with the Commanding Officer.	S.V.S. S.V.S.
ARRAS	Apl 25th		A.B.D Companies continued work on communication trenches. "C" Company worked on ARRAS defences & supplied 2 teams of miners for dugouts. Two N.C.Os on ARRAS defences & supplied 2 teams of miners for dugouts. One casualty wounded.	S.V.S
"	26th		as above	No casualties	S.V.S
"	27th		as above	Two casualties	S.V.S
"	28th		as above	One man wounded	S.V.S
"	29th		as above	No casualties	S.V.S
"	30th		as above	One man wounded	S.V.S

Pioneers 11 Liverpool
Vol 11
XIV
11.4
3 sheets

WAR DIARY

INTELLIGENCE SUMMARY

Army Form C. 2118.

Place	Date	Hour	Summary of Events and Information	Remarks and references to Appendices
ARRAS	May 1st		A.B.D Companies continued work on communications tunnels. "C" Company worked on ARRAS defences occupying Stays tunnels for dugouts. Five NCO's & men worked for 14th Division Signal Company.	
"	2nd		As above	as above Roclincourt	Clear
"	3rd		As above	As above	Clear
"	4th		As above	As above	Roclincourt	Clear
"	5th		As above	As above	Clear
"	6th		As above	As above	Roclincourt	Clear
"	7th		As above	As above	Roclincourt	Clear
"	8th		As above	as above	Roclincourt	Clear
"	9th		As above	As above. One man wounded	Clear
"	10th		As above	As above. Two men wounded	Clear
"	11th		As above	As above Roclincourt	Clear
"	12th		As above	As above. One man wounded	Clear
"	13th		As above	As above Roclincourt	Clear
"	14th		As above	As above Roclincourt	Clear

WAR DIARY or INTELLIGENCE SUMMARY.

Army Form C. 2118.

Place	Date	Hour	Summary of Events and Information	Remarks and references to Appendices
ARRAS	May 15		"C" Companies continued work on communication trenches. "C" Company worked on ARRAS defences & supplied two teams of miners for machine gun emplacements. One Officer & four other ranks content for Divisional Signal Company to Maroeuil.	Clear
"	16th		As above	no casualties	Fine
"	17th		As above	As above	Clear
"	18th		As above	Two casualties (3 slight wounds)	Clear
"	19th		As above	As above	Fine
"	20th		As above	no casualties	Fine
"	21st		As above	no casualties	Fine
"	22nd		As above	One wounded very slightly	Fine
"	23rd		As above	One wounded very slightly (abrasion)	Fine
"	24th		As above	One wounded.	Fine
"	25th		As above. A draft of 20 arrived. Two slightly wounded	Fine
"			As above	no casualties	Fine
"	25th		"A" & "D" Companies continued work on communication trenches "B" Company worked on ACHICOURT defences. "C" Company worked on ARRAS defences together with 60 men from Anthoine's & 9 3rd Army from the Engineers. One wounded	Clear

Army Form C. 2118.

WAR DIARY
or
INTELLIGENCE SUMMARY.
(Erase heading not required.)

Place	Date	Hour	Summary of Events and Information	Remarks and references to Appendices
ARRAS	26		A & D Companies continued work on communication trenches. B Company worked on ACHICOURT defences. C Company worked on ARRAS defences together with 60 O.R. from Battalion from H.Q. 3rd Bn. & 1 Officer from 8 Field Coy Engineers and 50 Infantry from 95th Inf. 5 Brigade. 2 other ranks wounded.	NIL
"	27th		As above	
"	28th		As above	No casualties
"	29		As above	Draft J.E.6 arrived strength 1 man died before reaching the Battalion. No casualties.
"	30th		As above	No casualties
"	31		As above	One man wounded

CONFIDENTIAL

War Diary
of

11th (S) Bn. The King's Liverpool Regt. (Pioneers)

From 1st June 1916
To 30th June 1916

(VOLUME XII)

11 Liverpools
Vol 12

12.Y.
(6 sheets)

XIV

WAR DIARY

INTELLIGENCE SUMMARY

(Erase heading not required.)

Army Form C. 2118.

Place	Date	Hour	Summary of Events and Information	Remarks and references to Appendices
ARRAS	June 1st		A & D Companies continued work on communication trenches. B Company worked on ACHICOURT defences, C Company worked on ARRAS defences together with 1 off & 60 OR from Northants Yeomy. 1 off & 30 ORs 89th Field Coy R.E. and 50 infantry from 95th Infy Brigade.	AA
"	2nd		As above. No casualties. 2nd Lieut V.T. Barby DSO rejoined battalion.	AA
"	3rd		As above. No casualties.	AA
"	4th		As above. No casualties.	AA
"	5th		As above but when Infantry from 95th Bde 2/S. A.G. Thomas wounded	AA
"	6th		As above. 2 Platoons "B" Coy worked in BONVILLE Defences. No casualties	AA
"	7th		As above. 4 other wounded, one severely	AA
"	8th		As above. One killed (Pte Goulding)	AA
"	9th		As above. No casualties	AA
"	10th		As above. No casualties	BBBB
"	11th		As above. No casualties	BBBB
"	12th		As above. No casualties	BBBB

Army Form C. 2118.

WAR DIARY
or
INTELLIGENCE SUMMARY.
(Erase heading not required.)

Instructions regarding War Diaries and Intelligence Summaries are contained in F. S. Regs., Part II. and the Staff Manual respectively. Title pages will be prepared in manuscript.

Place	Date	Hour	Summary of Events and Information	Remarks and references to Appendices
ARRAS	June 13th		A & D Companies worked on communication trenches. "B" Company had two platoons in RONVILLE defences & two platoons on ACHICOURT defences. "C" Company worked on ARRAS defences together with 70 men & 2 Officers 11th Royal Engineers & 10 men & 85 Engineers. No casualties	
"	14th		The whole Battalion were on Special work on front-line trenches. Several Officers attached Royal Engineers & Army Cyclist Corps worked on ARRAS defences	Nil
"	15th		The whole Battalion was on Special work in front-line trenches. One Officer & 10 men of Special Brigade of Engineers was attached to the 35th for Special work in first line trenches. The 35 Royal Engineers one Officer together with a party of the Army Cyclist Corps worked on ARRAS defences. There were no casualties	Nil
"	16th		B Company & a party of "D" Company worked on front line trenches. C Company found guides for carrying parties for front trenches. B Comp? worked on communication trenches & the remainder of "C" Coy together with a party from the Royal Engineers & Army Cyclist Corps worked on ARRAS defences. A further 50 Royal Engineers from Special Brigade were attached to the Battalion. There were no casualties	Nil

WAR DIARY or INTELLIGENCE SUMMARY.

Army Form C. 2118.

Place	Date	Hour	Summary of Events and Information	Remarks and references to Appendices
ARRAS	June 17th		"A" Company returned to work on communication trenches RONVILLE defences. "B" Company continued work on firing line. "C" Company worked on ARRAS defences together with 1 officer & 35 other ranks from Royal Engineers. Also a party of Army Cyclist Corps. "D" Company continued work on communication trenches & a "strong point." One officer & 1 other rank wounded.	
"	18th		"A" Company continued work on communication trenches. "B" Coy worked on RONVILLE defences. "C" Company worked on ARRAS defences together with a party of Army Cyclist Corps. No casualties. "D" Company worked on "strong point" & ACHICOURT defences.	
"	19th		"A" Company continued work on communication trenches. "B" Coy worked on RONVILLE & ACHICOURT defences. "C" Company worked on ARRAS defences together with a party of Army Cyclist Corps. "D" Coy were relieved in ACHICOURT & came into No 35 French barracks which took over the AGNY sector. D. & G. worked on ARRAS & billeted near French barracks.	
"	20th		"A" Company continued work on communication trenches. "B" Coy worked on RONVILLE & ACHICOURT defences. "C" Company worked on ARRAS defences together with Army Cyclist Corps. No casualties. "D" Coy a party of the Army Cyclist Corps. No casualties.	

WAR DIARY
INTELLIGENCE SUMMARY

Army Form C. 2118.

Place	Date	Hour	Summary of Events and Information	Remarks and references to Appendices
ARRAS	June 21st		"A" Company continued work on communication trenches. "B" by working on RIVILLE & ACHICOURT defences. "C" Company worked on ARRAS defences together with "D" Coy & a party of the Army Cyclist Corps. See Reverse.	
			Weather	
	22nd		As Above	Remark
			Orders were received that the Battalion would relieve Coys in the REDOUBT line on night of 23rd June.	
	23.		Officers of "C" & "D" Companies reconnoitered the Redoubt line as follows "A" Coy, Half Company & Proceeded to ACHICOURT the pioneer 2nd half "A" Coy Relieved ½ RONVILLE as pioneer relieving "A" Coy, Coy Relieved St SAUVEUR as pioneer relieving "B" Coy, Half Company of "B" Proceeded to St SAUVEUR as pioneer relieving a company of 5th Kings Shropshire Light Infantry. "C" Company one Platoon relieved 1 Platoon of Northumberland Fus: to the A.C. Corps. at DZ 617 on Map 1:40,000 51B France. One Platoon some Company relieved 1 Platoon Northumberland F. in Lower Redoubt. "D" Coy Relieved the Platoon M.H.B. Northern F.O. in the Nicolle Redoubt.	

WAR DIARY
INTELLIGENCE SUMMARY
(Erase heading not required.)

Army Form C. 2118.

Instructions regarding War Diaries and Intelligence Summaries are contained in F. S. Regs., Part II. and the Staff Manual respectively. Title pages will be prepared in manuscript.

Place	Date	Hour	Summary of Events and Information	Remarks and references to Appendices
ARRAS	May 23rd		Coy: One platoon "B" Coy relieved one platoon 12th Durham L.I. in the BOSCH REDOUBT. Headquarters two platoons "B" Coy, one platoon "C" Coy workshops ARRAS & DAINVILLE. Remainder in the Field Billets in Grenoble	Nil
ARRAS	24th		"C" & "B" sections of "D" Y.R. employment on the Rexem H.line as above. One platoon "B" Coy worked on ARRAS defences & one platoon "D" Coy carried material. No casualties.	Nil Nil
"	25th		As above	Nil
"	26th		Arrillery fire of Coys remained as the Redoubt line as above. One platoon of "C" Coy worked on ARRAS defences together with two platoons of "B" Coy.	Nil
"	27th		As above. No casualty.	Nil
"	28th		As above	Nil
"	29th		As above	Nil
"	30th		As above	Nil

July

11 Liverpools Vol 13

14

13.Y
(7 sheets)

Confidential
War Diary
of
11 Liverpools Regiment
(Pioneers)

From July 1st to July 31st 1916

(Volume 13)

CONFIDENTIAL

14th Division

EH3
31/7/16

Attached please find War Diary for the Battalion under my Command, from 1st July to 31st July 1916 (Vol XIII).

Please acknowledge receipt.

31/7/16

V. J. Iseley
Commdg. 14th (S) Bn. King's (Liverpool) (Pioneers)

<u>CONFIDENTIAL</u>

WAR DIARY

of

11th (S) Bn. The King's Liverpool Regt. (Pioneers)

From 1st July 1916
To 31st July 1916.

(Volume XIII)

V. J. Wailey, Lieut.-Colonel.
Commdg. 11th (S) Bn. King's Liverpool Regt. (Pioneers)

WAR DIARY
INTELLIGENCE SUMMARY
(Erase heading not required.)

Army Form C. 2118.

Place	Date	Hour	Summary of Events and Information	Remarks and references to Appendices
ARRAS	July 1st		A & B Companies & parts of C & D Coys remained in the billets line in ACHICOURT, RONVILLE, ST SAUVEUR, The CEMETRY OR WORKS FORESTIER, NICOLLS, & BOSKI REDOUBTS employment Since 1:40 p.m. 51st B.G.17 the Commander of C & D Coys worked on ARRAS defences. One Casualty	killed
"	2nd		As above	No Casualties	Killed
"	3rd		As above	Three Casualties	Wound
"	4th		As above	No Casualties	Killed
"	5th		As above	No Casualties	Killed
"	6th		As above	No Casualties	6/6/13
"	7th		As above	No Casualties	N.C.13
"	8th		As above	No Casualties	M.C.15
"	9th		As above	No Casualties	Killed
"	10th		As above	One Casualty	G. Car
"	11th		As above	No Casualties	W/Wd
"	12th		As above	No Casualties	Killed

Army Form C. 2118.

WAR DIARY
or
INTELLIGENCE SUMMARY.
(Erase heading not required.)

Place	Date	Hour	Summary of Events and Information	Remarks and references to Appendices
ARRAS	13th		A&B Companies as parts of 1 & 2 Companies remained in Billets, Platoons one in ACHICOURT, RIVILLE, ST SAUVEUR, THE CEMETERY, OIL WORKS, FORESTER NICOLLS & BOSKY REDOUBTS. Map reference trench 1:40,000 51.B.G.14. The remainder of C & D Companies worked on ARRAS defence, One casualty. Lt. QM. Callahan returned from leave. wounded	killed nil wounded 1
"	14th		As above	No casualties
"	15th		The Battalion was relieved from the Village & redoubts one by 6th & 8th Yorkshire Regiment & returned to their Billets in ARRAS. C & D Companies proceeded to the ROCLINCOURT sector & reported to two sub sectors to New work & the earth work. No casualties	Nil
"	16th		A, B, C Companies started work on new post line trench in the ROCLINCOURT sector. D Company worked on mine crater consolidation in No. 8 sub sector, i.e. about Highway between ROCLINCOURT & BAYOT. No Casualties	Nil
"	17th		A B C Companies continued work on post line trench as above & D Coy on consolidation of mine craters. No casualties	Nil
"	18th		As above	As above

Army Form C. 2118.

WAR DIARY
or
INTELLIGENCE SUMMARY.
(Erase heading not required.)

Instructions regarding War Diaries and Intelligence Summaries are contained in F. S. Regs., Part II. and the Staff Manual respectively. Title pages will be prepared in manuscript.

Place	Date	Hour	Summary of Events and Information	Remarks and references to Appendices
ARRAS	19th		A&C Companies continued work on new front line trenches on the ROCLINCOURT Sector. B Company in consolidation of mine craters. No casualties.	Fine
"	20th		As above. Aviation Activities. 2nd Lt Degeny & Clayton reported the Battalion.	Fine
"	21st		Lt Kent struck of strength temporarily for flying duties. Work Companies continued work on new front line trenches in the ROCLINCOURT Sector. B Company in consolidation of mine craters. No Casualties	Wet
"	22nd		As above	No Casualties
"	23rd		As above	No Casualties
"	24th		As above	Three Casualties
"	25th		As above	One Casualty
"	26th		The Battalion was relieved by the 14th & 18th Northumberland Fusiliers 21st Division & moved to ANZIN ST AUBIN. No Casualties.	Wet
"	27th		The Battalion moved to IVERGNY and went into billets at 4 p.m.	Wet

Five casualties were wounded accidentally, accidental or personal causes. One since reported died on 24th July.

Army Form C. 2118.

WAR DIARY
or
INTELLIGENCE SUMMARY.
(Erase heading not required.)

Instructions regarding War Diaries and Intelligence Summaries are contained in F. S. Regs., Part II. and the Staff Manual respectively. Title pages will be prepared in manuscript.

Place	Date	Hour	Summary of Events and Information	Remarks and references to Appendices
IVERGNY	28th		The Battalion remained in Billets. No Casualties	Nil
"	29th	Noon	The Battalion received order to move. Right half Battalion OUTREBOIS + Left half to FROHEN-le-GRAND arriving at their places at 3.30pm	Nil Nil
OUTREBOIS	30th		Right half Battalion remained in billets. No Casualties	Nil
FROHEN-le-GRAND			Left half Battalion remained in billets. No Casualties	Nil
OUTREBOIS FROHEN-le-GRAND	31st		Remained in Billets awaiting further instructions. No Casualties	Nil

Vol 14

14-Y
(9 sheets)

WAR DIARY OF

11th (S) Bn. The King's Liverpool Regt. (Pioneers)

FROM 1st August 1916
TO. 31st August 1916.

(Volume XIV.)

Army Form C. 2118.

WAR DIARY
or
INTELLIGENCE SUMMARY.
(Erase heading not required.)

Instructions regarding War Diaries and Intelligence Summaries are contained in F. S. Regs., Part II. and the Staff Manual respectively. Title pages will be prepared in manuscript.

Place	Date	Hour	Summary of Events and Information	Remarks and references to Appendices
	August			
BEAUMETZ	1st		Orders were received for the Battalion to move to BEAUMETZ arriving that	Nil
"	2nd		11 am & went into Billets. No Casualties. The Battalion remained in Billets & was inspected by the Commanding Officer. No Casualties.	Nil
"	3rd		The Battalion remained in Billets. Company Route marches in the morning. Inspection by Platoon Commanders in the afternoon.	Nil
"	4th		The Battalion remained in Billets. Companies were at work during the day.	Nil
"	5th		The Battalion remained in Billets. Company Training during the day.	Nil
"	6th		The Battalion remained in Billets & continued Company Training. Orders were received that Battalion would move on the 7th. The Transport left the Battalion to march to their new destination. Transport left DOM to march under 313rd Transport Officer & O.R.Sgt Obed	
"	7th		The Battalion proceeded in two parties of 2 battalions each to entraining point at CANDAS first party leaving Barn & clubraining at 5am the 2nd half leaving at Jam & entraining	

T/134. Wt. W708—776. 500000. 4/15. Sir J. C. & S.

WAR DIARY
or
~~INTELLIGENCE SUMMARY~~

(Erase heading not required.)

Army Form C. 2118.

Place	Date	Hour	Summary of Events and Information	Remarks and references to Appendices
1000 yds S.W. ALBERT			At camp, Relieving Station MERICOURT for Bath parties.	
Eg.a 7.8 France			Right half under Lt/Col Basté marched to Camp at Eg.a 7.8	
1.140,1/20,000 Sheet 62D			France Sheet 62D Edition I arriving at 4 p.m. Bivouacs to pitch Camp (tents). The left half under Major G.B. arrived	
	8th		At 4.30 p.m. The Young put across in Camp at 3.30 p.m. The Battalion remained in Camp Bayonet fighting, physical exercises & platoon drill during the day.	Glass
As above	9th		As above	Glass
As above	10th		As above	Glass
As above	11th		As above	Glass
As above	12th		The Battalion received orders to move to Fg.a Sheet 62D France 1:40,000. The Battalion moved out of its present Camp at 6.8 p.m. arriving in new Bivouac at 9.30 p.m. No Casualties. The Battalion relieved A Battalion of the Yorks & Lancs Regiment	Glass
Fg.a & Sheet 62D	13th		The Battalion remained in Bivouac at Fg.a. Silent working parties to Trenches near DELVILLE WOOD. Small parties took over Redoubts. No casualties.	Glass
As above			As above	Glass

WAR DIARY
or
INTELLIGENCE SUMMARY.

Army Form C. 2118.

Place	Date	Hour	Summary of Events and Information	Remarks and references to Appendices
Fq a Nveil 62D	14th		The Battalion remained in Bivouac & tents working parties to the trenches also to R.E. dumps & casualties	Wind West
as above	15th		as above	Wind West
as above	16th		as above	Wind West
Dacton	17th		O.C. B & C Coys Officers made necessary reconnaissance of positions etc to be followed to take up their positions for the forthcoming attack to take place on the 18th in which they together with the 61st & 62nd Bdy Royal Engineers would act as consolidating parties for Shrapnel's A Coy remained in Camp on RE dump fatigues the 5th men under L/Sgt. — working for the Divisional Signals. Two Casualties wounded accidentally	Wind
as above	18th	6.3am	B Coy moved off in 10 9 wagons to POMMERN REDOUBT taking 48 hours Lewis Gun & 6 Plunder for water	Wind
		8.30am	C Coy moved off in column of route together with two 9 Plunder for Lewis guns & water respectively. Both Companies were to remain in reserve until the former	

WAR DIARY
or
INTELLIGENCE SUMMARY.
(Erase heading not required.)

Army Form C. 2118.

Place	Date	Hour	Summary of Events and Information	Remarks and references to Appendices
79.a.Sud. 6.2.D Trench			at present held by the enemy had been captured. The companies were then reformed 3 assing parties each for strong points & then there were completed each company would find these parties	
1.c.1, etc?			to man the Redoubts. "B" Company were allotted to 3rd Brigade & "C" Coy to the 41st Brigade. The line in which the strong points were to be made was S.18.d.7.6. S.18.b.7. S.18.b.3½.9. S.17.D.6.7. S.17.D.3.7. S.17.c.5.9. but owing to the attack not succeeding at what S.18.c.10.7 S.18.b.13½.9 the two strong points could not be made. The remainder were moved to A & D Companies remained in camp	
Approx	19th	3.30	ready to move at half hours notice. All B & C Coy's had returned from the trenches except the Garrison of the four Strong Points & the casualties amounted to eleven killed thirty seven wounded. The Battalion less those ten strong points men during turkey to	(over)
			further casualty reports shared.	over
Asbonc	20th	7a	The whole of the Parties of the Strong points returned to camp. Casualties 6.4.7 am. killed 6 wounded 3 slightly wounded at duty	over

T.J134. Wt. W708-776. 500000. 4/15. Sir J.C. & S.

Army Form C. 2118.

WAR DIARY
or
INTELLIGENCE SUMMARY.
(Erase heading not required.)

Place	Date	Hour	Summary of Events and Information	Remarks and references to Appendices
T.A.C. Suzanne France 1:40,000	20th		The following Telegram was published in orders for 19th instant: "Following Message received from Corps Commander. The Army Commander has desired me to convey to you his congratulations on the successful work carried out by 14th Division yesterday. Commander & Staff of 33rd Army have also wired their congratulations."	Weu
			"A" Company worked on Support line in DELVILLE WOOD, "B" Coy worked on Support line S.E. of DELVILLE WOOD. "C" Company worked on communication trench running N.E. out of TRONES WOOD. "D" Coy found the usual R.E. parties for various workshops, & 50 men for tunnel Signal Company. One Casualty wounded	Weu
Wedroo	21st		"A" Company with "B" & "C" Coys. worked on communication trenches in vicinity of DELVILLE WOOD. "D" Coy found Signal Maton & R.E. parties. One casualty wounded.	Weu
As above	22nd		"A" Company took working parties in vicinity of DELVILLE WOOD. "B" & "C" Companies worked on communication trenches in the same area. "D" Company found usual R.E. fatigues. No Casualties	Weu

WAR DIARY or INTELLIGENCE SUMMARY.

Army Form C. 2118.

(Erase heading not required.)

Place	Date	Hour	Summary of Events and Information	Remarks and references to Appendices
t.g.a.	August 23rd		"A" Company worked on an assembly Trench in receipt of DELVILLE WOOD. "B" & "C" Coys worked on DELVILLE WOOD in communication	
Hill 63. D Punch			trenches & assembly trenches. "D" Company found working fatigues	
1.40, UTD			3 Casualties wounded	
As above	24th		"A" "B" "C" Coys proceeded to the vicinity of MALTZHORN & took up positions in order that they might be at hand to consolidate strongpoints for the attack to be made at 5.45 p.m. The Coys moved forward at about 9 pm & proceeded to work on strongpoints - consolidation of captured trenches. Casualties one killed, 3 wounded on active duty.	1 Killed
As above	25th	7pm	"B" & "C" Companies returned from work to mentioned on last	
		11am	"A" Coy worked in DELVILLE WOOD on fire & communication trenches. Two returned.	
As above	26th		"A" & "B" Companies worked on communication trenches in DELVILLE WOOD. "C" Company rested. "D" Coy found RE fatigues & repeat platoon 4 wounded three at duty, one missing.	

WAR DIARY
or
~~INTELLIGENCE SUMMARY.~~
(Erase heading not required.)

Army Form C. 2118.

Place	Date	Hour	Summary of Events and Information	Remarks and references to Appendices
79.a. Sheet 62D France 1/40,000	May 27th		"A" "B" & "C" Coys worked on communication trenches in vicinity of PEIZIERS WOOD. "D" Coy front signalling platoon & usual R.E. fatigues. One rifleman wounded on rifle at duty.	Appx A
	28th		Half of "A" "B" "D" & all "C" Company were employed on construction & improvement of communication trenches. The remaining half of "B" Coy found the signal platoon & R.E. parties. 2Lt Denny wounded, 6 casualties wounded & two killed O.R.	Appx B
Authie	29th		The Battalion rested in Bivouac except for small parties on R.E. dumps. Orders were received that the Battalion would move on 31st for march.	Appx C
Authie	30th		The Battalion was relieved by the Pioneer Battalion of 41st Division & moved to camp at T.8.b. 1/40,000 Thienne Authie's arrived there at 6 p.m.	Appx D
Authie	31st		Orders were received for the Battalion to entrain at MERICOURT at 11am. The Battalion proceeded by Rail KAIRAINES where it detrained & marched to TAILLY about pt 24 Sq 6K Sheet 3 France 1/250,000 where it arrived at 11pm & went into Billets.	Appx E

CONFIDENTIAL

WAR DIARY

OF

11TH. BN "THE KING'S" LIVERPOOL REGT (PIONEERS)

FROM 1st SEPTEMBER. 1916
TO 30TH. SEPTEMBER. 1916.

(VOLUME XV)

WAR DIARY
INTELLIGENCE SUMMARY

Army Form C. 2118.

Place	Date	Hour	Summary of Events and Information	Remarks and references to Appendices
September				
TATINGHEM	1st		The Battalion remained in Billets. Several new Billets were taken over cleaning up & general arrangements were made for training.	Clad
Dulpe 16	2nd		Billets were cleaned up & physical exercise & inspection parades were held.	Clad
As above	3rd	11am	Church parade. Inspection was made that officers & men had been properly fitted with boxers.	Clad
As above	4th	7.30	Physical Drill	Fine
		9-12	Commanding Officers inspection	
		2-3	Lecture by O.C. Companies to N.C.O's & listen to all officers below rank of Captain by Commanding Officer	Clad
As above	5th	9.7.30	Route march	Clad
		2-3	Foot inspection	
As above	6th		9 Officers proceeded on 48 hours leave to the country	Clad
			25 Other ranks proceeded on leave to England for 48 hours leave	
		7.7.30	Physical Drill	
		9-12	Motor Company & Squad drill	
As above	7th	7.7.30	Physical Drill	Clad
		9.15-12	Motor, Squads, Bombing & action training	

WAR DIARY

~~INTELLIGENCE~~ SUMMARY.
(Erase heading not required.)

Army Form C. 2118.

Place	Date	Hour	Summary of Events and Information	Remarks and references to Appendices
	August			
TALLY	8th	9.30	Route March.	
Rd maps		to 12	10 Officers & 20 other ranks proceeded to Rest Camp for 48 hrs	Steel
DIEPPE 16			Steel	
		2 - 3h	Foot inspection.	
as above	9th	7.30.5	Physical Drill	Steel
		9.30.12	Commanding Officers inspection.	
			Transport left for Camp 4 to N. of BERNACOURT to rest.	Nil
as above	10th	11h	Church Parade	Nil
as above	11th		Battalion Dinners. Entertainment at Divisional Kinema at AIRAINES.	Nil
BERNACOURT	12th		Battn. on Train. Arrived at Camp 4 to N. of BERNACOURT	Nil
	13th	4.30h	Battalion moved to FRICOURT WOOD Sheet 62D	Nil
FRICOURT WOOD 135			"A.C.D" Coys. billeted in the vicinity of DELVILLE WOOD "B" Coy supplied	Nil
as above	14th		the Battalion reserve. SP map S pts. Outposts - Diggins Shelters - Graft of Posts hastily entrenched	Nil
	15th	4.0h	The Battalion moved off by platoons to the road BERAFOY WOOD &	
			LONGUEVAL at map ref 140 Sq 12 Sheet 57 c 1:40,000 in order to rest	
			This road proved good for traffic when the attack had commenced	

WAR DIARY or INTELLIGENCE SUMMARY.

Army Form C. 2118.

(Erase heading not required.)

Instructions regarding War Diaries and Intelligence Summaries are contained in F.S. Regs., Part II. and the Staff Manual respectively. Title pages will be prepared in manuscript.

Place	Date	Hour	Summary of Events and Information	Remarks and references to Appendices
S.23.c.	July 15th		Lt. Hill 2nd Lt Boatman were wounded and 13 other ranks killed 39 wounded. Admitted to Hospital & wounded at duty other ranks the	Read
		1.40 a.m	Transport came up to MONTAUBAN at night.	Read
	16th	6.a.m	The Battalion continued work on the BERNAFAY WOOD & front.	Read
			140 S.R. Club 57 C. Casualties one killed & 3 wounded.	Read
		10 p.m	The Battalion moved back to FRICOURT WOOD arriving there at 12 M.N.	Read
FRICOURT WOOD D18.6 sheet 62D	17th-12 hrs		The Battalion moved to D.18.b. Sheet 62 D. Went arriving there at 4 p.m.	Read
	18th		The Battalion remained in camp resting. Strength of Battalion marched	Read
62.D.	19th		As above	Read
do	20th		As above	Read
do	21st		As above	Read
	22nd		The Battalion left camp at D.18.b by Bus for IVERGNY arriving there at 5 p.m.	Read
IVERGNY	23rd		The Battalion rested in billets	Read

WAR DIARY

Place	Date	Hour	Summary of Events and Information	Remarks and references to Appendices
IVERGNY	24th	10.50.	Church parade.	

The following orders were received by the Division.

Message from Commander in Chief begins. The first successes by the 4th Army on the 15th inst- are more satisfactory & have brought us a long step forward towards the final victory. The further advance yesterday (?) after such severe fighting was also a fine performance highly creditable to the troops, Staff Corps, Divisional & Brigade Staffs. Our new engine of war, the heavy section machine gun corps, acquitted itself splendidly on its first trial & has proved itself a very valuable addition to the Army. My warmest congratulations to Gen. the 4th Army on a very fine achievement.

The following telegram received from Fourth Army Commander, dated 23rd inst- to be with very great regret that I hear that 47th Division are leaving to Fourth Army, & before they do so, I desire to convey to every Officer & N.C.O. & man my gratitude & congratulations for the admirable work they have done. Both the DELVILLE WOOD & the attacks of the 15th & 16th Septr.

WAR DIARY
or
INTELLIGENCE SUMMARY

Army Form C. 2118.

Place	Date	Hour	Summary of Events and Information	Remarks and references to Appendices
	24th		They displayed a fighting spirit & a dash which is worthy of the best traditions of the British Army, whilst their discipline & Staff work of the has been beyond praise. The artillery support has on all occasions been adequate & well directed, and the morale of careful & thorough training I have been struck by the keenness & good comradeship which exist amongst all ranks in the 14th Division. It is a most valuable asset in other others that Both Staffs & Regimental Officers are working in harmony. It some future time should it may be my good fortune to again find them under my command. The following letter has been issued by the G.O.C. of the Division dated Oct 2nd. Sept. on completing our second tour of duty in the Battle of the SOMME he wishes to congratulate all ranks of the 14th (Light) Division on the high character they have earned for dash, discipline & hard work. The Division has proved that the New Army is to be every	

WAR DIARY
or
INTELLIGENCE SUMMARY.
(Erase heading not required.)

Army Form C. 2118.

Place	Date	Hour	Summary of Events and Information	Remarks and references to Appendices
	21st		Behind the old Army in fighting qualities & the nerves & the famous Regiments represented in the Division have, by the hardships endured & victories triumphantly made, acquired new & undying strength. The following order was received from XV Corps, in which the Division was & whilst in the Somme Battle.	
	24th		The 14th (Light) Division leaves the 5th Corps today. It was to capture Delville Wood. The Corps Commander wishes to Brig.Generals Commanding Brigades & indeed every Officer, N.C.O. & soldier, to very high esteem & have formed of the efficiency, discipline, moral, & fighting value of the Division. The clearing the Delville with the capture of HOP & ACH TRENCH between August 18th & 27th, & the attack of the SWITCH TRENCH & FLERS & beyond on September 15th were all difficult tasks, but the fine fighting spirit of the Division carried them all to a successful conclusion. The Division has accomplished everything which it has been called upon to perform & done it well. The	

WAR DIARY

Army Form C. 2118.

Place	Date	Hour	Summary of Events and Information	Remarks and references to Appendices
IVERGNY	25		It may being worth noting to be connected with for again. The Battalion rested in Billets	
IVERGNY	26		The Battalion received orders to move at 8am by Bus to WARLUS from where "A" Company proceeded to AGNY "B" Coy to Head Quarters of BERNEVILLE - "C" Coy to WARLUY "D" Coy to ARRAS. No Casualties	
BERNEVILLE As above	27		The Officer's reconnoitred the forward trenches where they were going to work. Power workshops formed at DAINVILLE	
As above	28		"A" Company commenced work on support & communication trenches in AGNY. "B" Company worked on communication trenches from ARRAS - DOULLENS Rd. Leaving. "C" Company worked on communication trenches around WAILY. "D" Coy in Support & communication trenches around RONVILLE. No Casualties	
As above	29		As above. Baatsre, Buftatas, B/Sgmt to TARRET to repair roads the	
As above	30		As above. No Casualties	

Confidential

WAR DIARY

OF

11th. BN. "THE KING'S" (LIVERPOOL) REGT. (PIONEERS.)

FROM. 1st October 1916
To. 31st October 1916.

(VOLUME XVI)

Army Form C. 2118.

WAR DIARY
or
INTELLIGENCE SUMMARY.
(Erase heading not required.)

Instructions regarding War Diaries and Intelligence Summaries are contained in F. S. Regs., Part II. and the Staff Manual respectively. Title pages will be prepared in manuscript.

Place	Date	Hour	Summary of Events and Information	Remarks and references to Appendices
October				
BERNEVILLE	1st		"A" Company worked on communication trenches in AGNY Sector	
			"B" Company worked on communication trenches from ARRAS-DOULLENS Rd Eastwards	
			"C" Company worked on communication trenches in WAILLY Sector	Ap1
			"D" Company worked on communication trenches in RONVILLE Area	Ap1
			No Casualties	Ap1
"	2nd		As above	As above
"	3rd		As above	One killed + one wounded Ap1
			Coy moved into ARRAS from "A" Sector	Ap1
"	4th		"A" Company worked on communication trenches in AGNY Sector	
			"B" Company worked on communication trenches + dugouts in RONVILLE	
			"C" Company on dugouts + communication trenches in WAILLY Sector	
			"D" Company worked on communication trenches in RONVILLE AREA	
			No casualties	Ap1
"	5th		As above	No casualties Ap1
"	6th		As above	No casualties Ap1

Army Form C. 2118.

WAR DIARY
~~INTELLIGENCE~~ SUMMARY.
(Erase heading not required.)

Instructions regarding War Diaries and Intelligence Summaries are contained in F. S. Regs., Part II. and the Staff Manual respectively. Title pages will be prepared in manuscript.

Place	Date	Hour	Summary of Events and Information	Remarks and references to Appendices
BERNEVILLE	7th		"A" Company worked on communication trenches in AGNY sector.	
			"B" Company worked on communication trenches in RONVILLE sector. "C" Company on dugouts & communication trenches in	
			WAILLY sector. "D" Company worked on communication trenches in	
			RONVILLE sector. No Casualties.	
"	8th		As above	As above	No Casualties	Wd
"	9th		As above	As above	No Casualties	Wd
"	10th		As above	As above	No Casualties	Wd
"	11th		As above	As above, No Casualties. Pte Roberts awarded Military Medal	Wd
"	12th		As above	As above, No casualties.	Wd
"	13th		As above	As above	No Casualties	Wd
"	14th		As above	As above	No Casualties	Wd
"	15th		As above	As above	No Casualties	Wd
"	16th		As above	As above. No Casualties	Wd
"	17th		As above	As above	No Casualties	Wd
"	18th		As above	As above	No Casualties	Wd

Army Form C. 2118.

WAR DIARY

~~INTELLIGENCE SUMMARY~~

(Erase heading not required.)

Instructions regarding War Diaries and Intelligence Summaries are contained in F.S. Regs., Part II. and the Staff Manual respectively. Title pages will be prepared in manuscript.

Place	Date	Hour	Summary of Events and Information	Remarks and references to Appendices
BERNEVILLE	19th		"A" Company worked on communication Trenches in AGNY sector	
"			"B" Company worked on communication Trenches dugouts in ~~F~~ BERNEVILLE sector	
"			"C" " " " " " " WAILLY sector	
"			"D" " " " " " in WAILLY sector. No casualties	
"	20th		As above as above No casualties	
"	21st		The whole Battalion eased work. The above & B&D Companies came	
			Killed at Berneville A&C Companies remained in their billets. No casualties	Nil
"	22nd		The whole Battalion worked on carrying "Accessories" in "F" sector WAILLY.	Nil
			No casualties.	
"	23rd		As above as above No casualties.	Nil
"	24th		As above as above No casualties.	Nil
"	25th		As above as above No casualties.	Nil
"	26th		The Battalion rested in Billets.	Nil
"	27th		"A" & "C" Companies moved in AGNY & WAILLY worked on communication	
			Trenches & dugouts.	
			"B" Company worked on C. Trenches for ARRAS-DOULLENS Rd eastwards. "D" Company	
			returned to billets in ARRAS. No casualties	Nil

WAR DIARY
INTELLIGENCE SUMMARY.
(Erase heading not required.)

Army Form C. 2118.

Place	Date	Hour	Summary of Events and Information	Remarks and references to Appendices
BERNEVILLE	Oct 28th		"A" & "C" Companies worked on communication trenches & dugouts in AGNY & WAILLY respectively	
			"B" Company worked on communication trenches from ARRAS - DOULLENS Rd eastwards	Nil
			"D" Company worked on dugouts in RONVILLE - ACHICOURT Sector. No casualties	Nil
"	29th		As above. No casualties	Nil
"	30th		As above	
			Returned from commanding H.Q. 1st & 3rd Inf. Brigade Lt. Col. BAIRD D.S.O.	Nil
"	31st		"A" & "C" Companies worked on communication trenches & dugouts in AGNY & WAILLY respectively. "B" Company worked on communication trenches from ARRAS - DOULLENS Rd eastwards. "D" Company worked on dugouts in RONVILLE - ACHICOURT Sector. One casualty wounded.	Nil

17-Y
6 sheets

Vol 17

CONFIDENTIAL.

WAR DIARY
OF
11TH. BN "THE KING'S" (LIVERPOOL) REGT (PIONEERS)

FROM. 1st NOVEMBER. 1916
TO   30TH NOVEMBER. 1916

(VOLUME XVII)

Army Form C. 2118.

WAR DIARY
or
INTELLIGENCE SUMMARY
(Erase heading not required.)

Instructions regarding War Diaries and Intelligence Summaries are contained in F. S. Regs., Part II. and the Staff Manual respectively. Title pages will be prepared in manuscript.

Place	Date	Hour	Summary of Events and Information	Remarks and references to Appendices
	November			
BERNEVILLE	1st		"A" Company worked on communication trenches in AGNY Sector	
			"B" Company 9.200 yds from the Infantry worked on communication trenches from ARRAS-DOULLENS Rd. Southward.	
			"C" Company worked on communication trench adjacent to the WAILLY Sector.	
			"D" Company worked on Defences in the RONVILLE - ACHICOURT Ave. No Casualties	
	2nd		As above	No Casualties
	3rd		As above	No Casualties
	4th		As above	No Casualties
	5th		Orders were received for the Battalion to move to GOUY-EN-ARTOIS. Was relieved by the 5th Northamptonshire Regiment in the various sectors & marched by Coys in daylight to GOUY-en-ARTOIS to huts. No Casualties.	
GOUY-n-ARTOIS	6th		The Battalion remained in huts. Coys went by Companies baths	
"	7th		"	"

Army Form C. 2118.

WAR DIARY
or
INTELLIGENCE SUMMARY.
(Erase heading not required.)

Instructions regarding War Diaries and Intelligence Summaries are contained in F. S. Regs., Part II. and the Staff Manual respectively. Title pages will be prepared in manuscript.

Place	Date	Hour	Summary of Events and Information	Remarks and references to Appendices
GOUY-EN-ARTOIS	8th		The Battalion proceeded by French Rail to BUNEVILLE arriving there at 3pm.	
BUNEVILLE	9th		The Commanding Officer inspected billets.	
"	10th		Companies carried on coy training	
"	11th		As above. Draft of 8 O.R. arrived	
"	12th	2-5	Physical Drill.	
	9-12	Squad, platoon, coy drill	
	2-3	Lectures. Rev Hotten Gas arrangement. Also repairs to arms etc.	
"	13th		As above	
			As above	
"	14th		Men went on detachment testing hurdles	
"	15th	7-8	Physical drill	
	9-12	Squad, platoon, coy drill. The Coy used rifle range, bombing ground & Lewis gun rack.	
"	16th		As above	
"	17th		As above	
"	18th		As above	

WAR DIARY or INTELLIGENCE SUMMARY.

Army Form C. 2118.

Place	Date	Hour	Summary of Events and Information	Remarks and references to Appendices
Bruneville	19th	7.0	Physical Drill	
Bruneville		9-12	Squad drill, Bombing, Rifle Range & Lewis gun instruction	
Bruneville		3.30	"B" Coy & 50 men of "A" Coy were moved into ARRAS for work under 12th Division	Wed
"	20th	7-0	Physical Drill	
"		9-12	Squad drill, platoon & coy drill, Bombing, Rifle Range & Lewis gun instruction	V/Sh1
"	21st	-	As above. Battalion Runners being trained for Competition	V/Sh1
"	22nd	-	As above " " "	V/Sh1
"	23rd	"	As above & in addition improvements to barns etc are being carried out.	V.2.13.
"	24th	"	As above: 1. Officer & 5 other Ranks A Coy proceeded by Motor Lorries to ARRAS for work there.	V.2.12.
"	25th	"	Inspection of Billets by Commanding Officer.	V.2.13.
"	26th	-	Church Parade in morning; Football match in afternoon	V.2.13.
"	27th		Lieut. Coll V J Bailey to S.O w/ to take the pony command of 42nd Inf. Brigade. Lewis gun and Bombing Instruction carried out.	CEO

Army Form C. 2118.

WAR DIARY
or
INTELLIGENCE SUMMARY.
(Erase heading not required.)

Instructions regarding War Diaries and Intelligence Summaries are contained in F.S. Regs., Part II. and the Staff Manual respectively. Title pages will be prepared in manuscript.

Place	Date	Hour	Summary of Events and Information	Remarks and references to Appendices
BUIRE VILLE	28th	10 am	Smell Box Respirators issued to C Coy. Ordinary routine carried out.	BC5
"	29th	10 am	Do. Do. Do.	EC6
"	30th		Ordinary Routine Continued. Runners race at Bri[gade] H.Q. Bn. Football match. D v HQ. Lieut. Col. V.J. Bailey D.S.O. rejoined and takes over Command of Battn.	EC26

CONFIDENTIAL

Vol 18

18.Y
5 sheets

WAR DIARY

OF

11TH BN. THE KING'S LIVERPOOL REGT (PIONEERS)

FROM   1st December 1916
TO   31st December 1916

(VOLUME XVIII)

WAR DIARY or INTELLIGENCE SUMMARY

Army Form C. 2118.

Place	Date	Hour	Summary of Events and Information	Remarks and references to Appendices
Burcoville	Decr 1/16	1st	Head-Quarters were fitted with Small Box Respirators. The usual training of the Battalion was carried out i.e. Physical Drill, musketry, Lewis gun, Bombing.	V.J.B.
"	2nd		A and B Coys on Detachment in ARRAS, were relieved by C and D Coys. The Relief being carried out by motor Lorries	V.J.B.
"	3rd		C & D Coys on detachment in the ARRAS sector, as detachment to A Coy supplied parts for work in the village & 50 men for work in making hurdles. Three casualties wounded.	
"	4th		Do. above	to casualties Killed
"	5th		As above	to casualties Wounded
"	6th		As above	to casualties Killed
"	7th		As above	to casualties Killed
"	8th		As above	to casualties Killed
"	9th		As above	Andrew 6 casualty Killed
"	10th		As above	As above two casualties Killed
"	11th		As above	As above No Casualty Killed
0h8	12th		As above	As above No Casualty Killed

WAR DIARY

INTELLIGENCE SUMMARY

Army Form C. 2118.

Place	Date	Hour	Summary of Events and Information	Remarks and references to Appendices
Berneville	13th		C & D Coys worked in ARRAS on attachment.	
"	"		B Coy supplied parties to work in the village & 50 other ranks on attachment making trench latrines.	
"	14th		As above	Wind & fine
"	15th		As above	Showers/Rain
"	16th		As above	Showers/Rain
"	17th		The Battalion ten Coys moved to DAINVILLE by march for Training	Wind
"			Hrs at 2 noon. C & D Coys remain in ARRAS, 50 men apart for making huts. Lt. Col. Bailey left to take command of Reserve Infantry Battalion	Wind
DAINVILLE	18th		The Battalion moved from DAINVILLE to BERNEVILLE	Wind
Berneville	19th		The Battalion relieved the 5th Northum. Fus. B/12 Pioneer Battn. at Le FERMONT	Wind
"	20th		A Coy & HQrs at BERNEVILLE. B Coy at Le FERMONT. D Coy in ARRAS. C Coy in AGNY	Wind
"	21st		"A" Coy worked on communication trenches from ARRAS-DOULLENS R. returned. "B" Coy worked on communication trenches to the FERMONT sector. "C" Coy worked on trenches in AGNY sector. "D" Coy worked on trenches in RONVILLE sector. Three casualties	

One officer of D.O.R.

Army Form C. 2118.

WAR DIARY
of
INTELLIGENCE SUMMARY.
(Erase heading not required.)

Place	Date	Hour	Summary of Events and Information	Remarks and references to Appendices
BERNEVILLE	22nd		"A" Coy worked on communication trench from ARRAS-DOULLENS Rd. Westwards. "B" Coy worked on communication trench to the BERMONT tube to "C" Coy worked on communication trench in "G" sector. "D" Coy worked on communication trench 4 dugouts in FAYEULLE sector. Workshops formed at Dainville	
"	23rd		As above	Elet
"	24th		As above	Elet
"	25th		As above	Elet
"	26th		As above	Elet
"	27th		As above	Elet
"	28th		As above	Elet
"	29th		As above	Elet
"	30th		As above	Elet
"	31st		As above	Elet

CONFIDENTIAL

Vol 19

WAR DIARY

OF

11TH. BN "THE KING'S" (LIVERPOOL) REGT (PIONEERS)
T4

FROM 1st JANUARY 1917 TO 31st JANUARY 1917

(VOLUME XIX)

CONFIDENTIAL

CONFIDENTIAL

11th BATTALION,
THE KING'S LIVERPOOL
REGIMENT (PIONEERS).
No. C.13/a
Date. 1-2-17

14th Division

I herewith forward War Diary of the Battn under my Command for Jany 1917 (Vol XIX).

Please acknowledge receipt

1/2/17

E C Ogle Major
Commandg
11th (S) Bn. The King's Liverpool Regt. (Pioneers)

WAR DIARY
INTELLIGENCE SUMMARY.
(Erase heading not required.)

Army Form C. 2118.

Place	Date	Hour	Summary of Events and Information	Remarks and references to Appendices
BERNEVILLE	Jan. 1917 1st		"A" Coy worked on communication trenches from ARRAS-DOULLENS Road Eastwards, "B" Coy worked on communication trenches in the le FERMONT Sector, "C" Coy worked on communication trenches & dugouts in "G" Sector "D" Coy worked on communication trenches & dugouts in RONVILLE Sector. Workshops at Wanville carried on. No casualties.	Wd.
"	2nd		As above	No casualties. Wd.
"	3rd		As above	No casualties. Wd.
"	4th		As above	No casualties. Wd.
"	5th		As above	No casualties. Wd.
"	6th		As above	No casualties. Wd.
"	7th		As above	No casualties. Wd.
"	8th		As above	No casualties. Wd.
"	9th		As above	No casualties. Wd.
"	10th		As above	No casualties. Wd.
"	11th		As above	No casualties. Wd.
"	12th		As above	No casualties. Wd.

Army Form C. 2118.

WAR DIARY
~~INTELLIGENCE~~ SUMMARY.
(Erase heading not required.)

Instructions regarding War Diaries and Intelligence Summaries are contained in F.S. Regs., Part II. and the Staff Manual respectively. Title pages will be prepared in manuscript.

Place	Date	Hour	Summary of Events and Information	Remarks and references to Appendices
BERNEVILLE	Jan 13th		"A" Coy worked on communication trenches from ARRAS-DOULLENS Rd Eastwards. B Coy worked on communication trenches on the Le FERMONT Sector. "C" Coy worked on communication trench Leps in "G" sector. "D" Coy worked on communication trench dugouts in RONVILLE Posts	
"	14th		Workships were carried on work at Berneville. As above	
"	15th		"A" Coy moved to GOUY-EN-ARTOIS. Knots worth "B" Coy worked on communication trenches in the le Fermont sector. "C" Coy moved to Le FERMONT sector. "D" Coy worked on communication trench dugouts in RONVILLE sector. Workshops at Berneville as usual. No casualties.	
"	16th		"B" & "C" Coys worked on construction of trenches. No Casualties	
"	17th		"D" Coy worked on Roads "B" & "C" Coys worked as on 15th inst continued work as on 15th inst. No casualties	
"	18th		As above. Lyn Casualties As above. No Casualties	
"	19th		"A" Coy worked on Roads. "B" Coy worked on Leps & communication trenches near to AGNY. "D" Coy trench dugouts & C.T. to Lyrapele Miles	

WAR DIARY / INTELLIGENCE SUMMARY

Army Form C. 2118.

(Erase heading not required.)

Instructions regarding War Diaries and Intelligence Summaries are contained in F. S. Regs., Part II. and the Staff Manual respectively. Title pages will be prepared in manuscript.

Place	Date	Hour	Summary of Events and Information	Remarks and references to Appendices
BERNEVILLE	Jan. 20th		"A" Coy worked on Ryall's Av. "B" Coy worked on Communication Trench Adepot. "C" Coy worked on Cape Communication Trench in the REAR area. "D" Coy worked on supports & Communication Trench in the FONCVILLE area. No casualties	Nil
"	21st		As above. No casualties	Nil
"	22nd		As above. No casualties	Nil
"	23rd		As above. No casualties	Nil
"	24th		As above. No casualties	Nil
"	25th		As above. No casualties	Nil
"	26th		As above. No casualties	Nil
"	27th		As above. No casualties	Nil
"	28th		As above. Reinforcement to O.R.	Nil
Do	29th		As above. One Casualty	Nil
"	30th		As above. Ration Fatigues moved to Granville Camp.	Nil
"	31st		As above. No casualties	Nil

109 Other Reinforcements joined during the month. 2nd Lt. L. W. Mendes-Frankworth Williams, Randolph, Hallatt, Davey, Ayley, Westrup, Rew, Horrocks.

CONFIDENTIAL

WAR DIARY

OF

11TH (S) BN. "THE KING'S" (LIVERPOOL) REGIMENT.
(PIONEERS).

From: 1st February 1917.

To: 28th February 1917.

(Volume XX)

CONFIDENTIAL

11th Division

Herewith War Diary for the Battalion under my Command, from 1-2-17 to 28-2-17. (Vol XX). Please acknowledge Receipt.

1/3/17

E.C. Ogle Lieut.-Colonel
Commdg. 11th (S) Bn. King's Liverpool Regt. (Pioneers)

WAR DIARY or INTELLIGENCE SUMMARY

Army Form C. 2118.

Place	Date	Hour	Summary of Events and Information	Remarks and references to Appendices
DAINVILLE	Feb 1st		HQ at Dainville. "A" Coy worked at [illeg.] "GOUY-EN-ARTOIS", "B" Coy worked in the LEFERMONT Sector. "C" Coy worked on the AGNY Sector. "D" Coy worked on RONVILLE Sector. Fortification of sector. No Casualties.	Weather Wet
"	2nd		As above	Wet
"	3rd		HQ at Dainville. "A" Coy worked at GOUY-EN-ARTOIS. "B" Coy moved into ARRAS. "C" Coy worked on the AGNY Sector & "D" Coy worked on the Ronville Sector on dug-outs, saps, & communication trenches. No Casualties.	Wet
"	4th		HQ at Dainville. "A" Coy mortar on repairs at GOUY-EN-ARTOIS. "B" Coy worked in ARRAS. "C" Coy worked on AGNY sector. "D" Coy worked in Ronville sector. No Casualties	Wet
ARRAS	5th		HQ moved to ARRAS. "A" Coy worked at GOUY. "B" Coy worked in ARRAS. "C" Coy worked in AGNY sector. "D" Coy worked in RONVILLE Sector. No casualties. One Other Rank slightly wounded (remained for duty)	Wet
ARRAS	6th		HQ at ARRAS. "B" Coy moved into the billets in ARRAS. The Coys worked in ARRAS, RONVILLE sector & AGNY as above. One casualty wounded.	Wet
"	7th		HQ "B" C" in ARRAS. "A" Coy worked in RONVILLE sector. "D" Coy moved to ARRAS. Same areas as remarked before/February No casualties.	G. Glad
"	8th		"A" "B" "C" "D" Coys worked in Ronville area on dug-outs & communication trenches. No casualties.	Wet
"	9th		As above	Clear

WAR DIARY or INTELLIGENCE SUMMARY

Army Form C. 2118.

Place	Date	Hour	Summary of Events and Information	Remarks and references to Appendices
ARRAS.	10th		A B C D Coys worked in Ronville area. A reconnoitring HAVANNAH B in trenches S.E. of ARRAS; C mine dugout in stores. D TM en place etc. No casualties. A Coy commenced work on emplacements	S/P.
	11th		Same as yesterday; no casualties.	
	12th		As yesterday; no casualties	H.
	13th		As yesterday; no casualties.	
	14th		As above. No casualties	
	15th		As above. Successively slightly wounded.	WM
	16th		As above. No casualties.	
	17th		As above. No casualties	Wed
	18th		As above. E. Pl. & Lt. H. GARNHAM joined the Battalion. No casualties	Wed
	19th		As above. No casualties	Wed
	20th		As above. No casualties	Wed
	21st		As above. No casualties	Wed
	22nd		As above. No casualties	Wed
	23rd		As above. No casualties	Wed
	24th		As above. No casualties	Wed
	25th		As above. No casualties	Wed
	26th		As above. No casualties	Wed
	27th		As above. No casualties	Wed
	28th		As above. No casualties	H.W.

CONFIDENTIAL.

WAR DIARY

OF

11TH. BN. "THE KING'S" (LIVERPOOL) REGT, (PIONEERS)

FROM :- 1st MARCH. 1917.
TO :- 31st MARCH. 1917.

(VOLUME XXI).

Army Form C. 2118.

WAR DIARY
or
INTELLIGENCE SUMMARY

(Erase heading not required.)

Instructions regarding War Diaries and Intelligence Summaries are contained in F. S. Regs., Part II. and the Staff Manual respectively. Title pages will be prepared in manuscript.

Place	Date 1917	Hour	Summary of Events and Information	Remarks and references to Appendices
ARRAS	March 1st		"A" Coy worked on T.M. Em. RONVILLE area, "B" Coy on circular trench round ARRAS, and TM Em. RONVILLE area, "C" Coy on Left Bn HQ Dugout, RONVILLE area, "D" Coy on Right Bn HQ Dugout, RONVILLE area. No casualties	H.H.
"	2nd		As above. No casualties	H.H.
"	3rd		" " In addition "A" Coy repaired ARRAS – DOULLENS road. No casualties	H.H.
"	4th		" " "B" Coy repaired ARRAS – ACHICOURT road. No casualties	H.H.
"	5th		As above. No work on roads. No casualties	H.H.
"	6th		As above. No casualties	H.H.
"	7th		As above. In addition "A" Coy repaired ARRAS – DOULLENS road. No casualties	H.H.
"	8th		As above. No work on roads. No casualties	H.H.
"	9th		As above. In addition "A" Coy repaired ARRAS – DOULLENS road. No casualties " " also worked on HAVELOCK EXTENSION. No casualties	H.H.
"	10th		As above. In addition "A" Coy repaired ARRAS – DOULLENS road. No work on HAVELOCK EXTENSION. No casualties	H.H.
"	11th		As above. No casualties	H.H.
"	12th		As above. In addition "A" Coy repaired ARRAS – DOULLENS road, and worked on HAVELOCK RIGHT. No casualties	H.H.
"	13th		As above. "A" Coy repaired ARRAS – DOULLENS road. No work on HAVELOCK EXTENSION. Four casualties (1 killed, 3 wounded).	H.H.
"	14th		As above. "A" Coy repaired ARRAS – DOULLENS road. No casualties	H.H.
"	15th		As above. " " " " One casualty (slightly wounded)	H.H.

Army Form C. 2118.

WAR DIARY
or
INTELLIGENCE SUMMARY

(Erase heading not required.)

Place	Date 1917	Hour	Summary of Events and Information	Remarks and references to Appendices
ARRAS	March 16		"A" Coy worked on T.M. Bn RONVILLE area, and rehaired ARRAS–DOULLENS road. "B" Coy on circular trench round ARRAS and T.M. Bn RONVILLE area. "C" Coy on Left Bn H.Q. Dugout, RONVILLE area. "D" Coy on Right Bn HQ Dugout and C.T. RONVILLE area. One casualty (wounded)	W.H.
"	17th		"A" Coy worked on C.T. RONVILLE area and rehaired ARRAS–DOULLENS Road. Remainder as yesterday. One casualty (wounded)	W.H.
"	18th		"A" Coy worked on roads S.E. of RONVILLE and ARRAS–DOULLENS road. "B" Coy on RONVILLE road to old German front line and Sap X 15. "C" Coy and "D" Coy on C.T. from our old front line to old German front line. Two casualties (wounded)	W.H.
"	19th		As above except "C" Coy worked on new front line. No casualties.	W.H.
"	20th		"A" C & B Coy worked on roads S.E. of RONVILLE and ARRAS–DOULLENS road. "C" Coy on new front line, also on Bde Dugout. "D" Coy on Cable trench. Two casualties {one killed, one wounded}	W.H.
"	21st		As above. No casualties	W.H.
"	22nd		"A" & "B" Coy worked on roads SE of RONVILLE and ARRAS–DOULLENS road. "C" Coy on Bde Dugout and C.T. "D" Coy on C.T. No casualties	W.H.
"	23rd		As above. Five casualties (1 killed 4 wounded)	W.H.
"	24th		As above. No casualties	W.H.
"	25th		As above. No casualties	W.H.
"	26th		As above. No casualties	W.H.
"	27th		As above. Eleven casualties (1 killed 10 wounded)	W.H.
"	28th		As above. No casualties	W.H.
"	29th		As above. No casualties	W.H.
"	30th		As above. No casualties	W.H.
"	31st		As above. No casualties	W.H.

CONFIDENTIAL 22 Y
5 sheets

Vol 22

WAR DIARY

OF

11th (S) Bn. The King's Liverpool Regt. (Pioneers)

FROM 1st April 1917
TO 30th April 1917.

(VOLUME) XXII.

Army Form C. 2118.

WAR DIARY
or
INTELLIGENCE SUMMARY

(Erase heading not required.)

Instructions regarding War Diaries and Intelligence Summaries are contained in F.S. Regs., Part II. and the Staff Manual respectively. Title pages will be prepared in manuscript.

Place	Date	Hour	Summary of Events and Information	Remarks and references to Appendices
ARRAS	April 1917		"A" & "B" Coys worked on roads SE of RONVILLE and ARRAS-DOULLENS road.	
	1		"C" & "D" " on C.T.s and assembly trenches. No casualties	H.H.
"	2nd		As above. No casualties	H.H. H.H.
"	3rd		As above. No casualties	H.H. H.H.
"	4th		As above (2 platoons "A" attached to R.A.) Reinforcements 26 O.Rs	H.H. H.H.
"	5th		As above. Eight casualties. (1 wounded) C & D Coy on G.S. Wagon roads. Eleven casualties	H.H. H.H.
			"A" Coy worked on roads SE of RONVILLE and ARRAS-DOULLENS road.	
			C.T.s and assembly trenches. "B" Coy commenced Rly. tracks. Eleven casualties	
"	6th		(1 killed, 4 wounded, 2 wounded and gassed, 4 gassed)	H.H. H.H.
"	7th		Work as above. 4 casualties (3 wounded, 1 shell shock). Reinforcement 38 O.R's	H.H. H.H.
"	8th		Work as above. No casualties	H.H. H.H.
			"A" Coy worked on roads SE of RONVILLE and ARRAS-DOULLENS road. "B" Coy	
			continued work on GS Wagon Tracks. "C" & "D" Coys rested. 3 casualties (wounded)	
"	9th		"B" Coy and 2 Platoons "A" Coy made Wagon roads. "D" Coy made Mule tracks.	H.H. H.H.
			"C" Coy made Fire Trench. One casualty (wounded) Reinforcements 2 O.R's.	
"	10		As above except "C" Coy worked on roads NEUVILLE VITASSE. No casualties	H.H. H.H.

Complimentary Order by Major-General V. Couper

The Commander-in-Chief has personally requested me to convey to all ranks of the 14th (Light) Division, his high opinion of the excellent fighting qualities shown by the Division.

The commencement of the great offensive of 1917 has been marked by an initial success in which more than 11,000 prisoners and 100 guns have been taken on the first day alone.

The Division has taken a prominent part in achieving this success and maintained the reputation gained last year on the SOMME, and added to the laurels of the gallant regiments of which it is composed.

1577 Wt. W10791/1773 500,000 1/15 D.D.&L. A.D.S.S./Forms/C. 2118.

WAR DIARY
INTELLIGENCE SUMMARY
(Erase heading not required.)

Army Form C. 2118.

Place	Date 1917	Hour	Summary of Events and Information	Remarks and references to Appendices
ARRAS	11		"B" Coy, "D" Coy & Remainder of "A" Coy worked on roads BEAURAINS - TILLOY and TILLOY - WANCOURT. "C" Coy rested. No casualties	N. N. N. N. N. N. N. N. N. N. N.
DAINVILLE	12		The Battalion moved from ARRAS to DAINVILLE.	
HABARCQ	13		" " " DAINVILLE to HABARCQ.	
GRAND RULLECOURT	14		" " " HABARCQ to GRAND RULLECOURT	N. N.
			COMPLIMENTARY ORDER	
			Copy of letter from VII Corps. "As the 14th (Light) Division is leaving the Corps for a well earned rest, the Corps Commander takes the opportunity of congratulating you and all in your command on the manner in which they have conducted themselves during the victorious advance. The Division, not only by its spirited advance, but by the hard work put in previously, has added to its long list of honours. The Corps Commander wishes the Division the best of luck and hopes he will be fortunate enough to soon again include such a hard fighting Division in his command.	
	15		The Battalion rested in billets	N. N. N. N. N. N. N.
	16		" " " " " "	N. N. N. N. N. N. N.
	17		" " " " " "	
	18		" " " " " " (Coy's carried out training)	
	19		" " " " " " " "	
	20		" " " " " " " "	
	21		" " " " " " " "	
	22		" " " " " " (Church Parade)	

Army Form C. 2118.

WAR DIARY
or
INTELLIGENCE SUMMARY.
(Erase heading not required.)

Instructions regarding War Diaries and Intelligence Summaries are contained in F.S. Regs., Part II. and the Staff Manual respectively. Title pages will be prepared in manuscript.

Place	Date April 1917	Hour	Summary of Events and Information	Remarks and references to Appendices
GRAND RULLECOURT	23		The Battalion moved from GRAND RULLECOURT to POMMIER.	W. D.
POMMIER	24		" " " POMMIER to BAILLEULMONT. Capt H R Bennett and Capt M.C.M Dennt rejoined. Reinforcements. 6 ORs	W. D.
BAILLEULMONT	25		The Battalion rested in billets.	W. D.
"	26		" " "	W. D.
"	27		The Battalion moved from BAILLEULMONT to ARRAS.	W. D.
ARRAS	28		"C" Coy worked on TILLOY - WANCOURT road, "D" Coy on Wagon tracks BEAURAINS - TILLOY, (GUEMAPPE area.) "A" & "B" Coys worked on assembly trenches. 2 casualties (wounded)	W. D.
"	29		The Battalion moved into bivouacs on TELEGRAPH HILL. Coys continued work as yesterday. 2 casualties (wounded)	W. D.
TELEGRAPH HILL	30		"C" Coy worked on TILLOY - WANCOURT road, "D" Coy on Wagon tracks BEAURAINS - TILLOY, (GUEMAPPE area.) "A" & "B" Coys worked on assembly trenches. No casualties and TILLOY - WANCOURT. Reinforcements 1. O.R.	W. D.

CONFIDENTIAL

Vol 23

23.Y.
5 sheets

WAR. DIARY.

OF.

11TH. BN THE KING'S (LIVERPOOL) REGT. (PIONEERS)

FROM.   1st MAY. 1917
TO   31st MAY. 1917.

(VOLUME. XXIII)

CONFIDENTIAL

Army Form C. 2118.

WAR DIARY

INTELLIGENCE SUMMARY

(Erase heading not required.)

Instructions regarding War Diaries and Intelligence Summaries are contained in F. S. Regs., Part II. and the Staff Manual respectively. Title pages will be prepared in manuscript.

Place	Date	Hour	Summary of Events and Information	Remarks and references to Appendices
TELEGRAPH HILL.	May 1917 1st		"C" Coy worked on TILLOY - WANCOURT road. "D" Coy on Wagon Tracks BEAURAINS - TILLOY and TILLOY - WANCOURT. "A" & "B" Coys worked on assembly trenches GUÉMAPPE area. No casualties.	N.H.
	2nd		"C" Coy worked on TILLOY - WANCOURT road. "D" Coy carried for R.Es. "A" & "B" Coys rested. One casualty (wounded)	N.H.
	3rd		Adv H. Qrs and the Companies moved forward to the WANCOURT area. Work could not be proceeded with owing to the situation. One casualty (wounded)	N.H.
	4th		"A" & "B" Coys dug C.Ts in WANCOURT area. "D" Coy made lorry & wagon tracks to R.E dump on TILLOY - WANCOURT road. "C" Coy rested. One casualty (wounded)	N.H.
	5th		"A" & "B" Coys dug C.Ts. in GUÉMAPPE area. "D" Coy made corduroy track to R.E dump on TILLOY - WANCOURT road. "C" Coy repaired TILLOY - WANCOURT road. Eleven casualties (wounded)	N.H.
	6th		"A" & "B" Coys dug C.Ts. in GUÉMAPPE area. "C" Coy worked on TILLOY - WANCOURT road. "D" Coy worked on CORPS LINE in WANCOURT area. Three casualties. (Capt H.R. Bennett and 2 O.Rs wounded)	N.H.
	7th		Work as above. No casualties (Reinforcements 4 O.Rs)	N.H.
	8th		Work as above. Four casualties (2nd Lt J Acheson & 3 O Rs wounded)	N.H.
	9th		Work as above. One casualty (killed)	N.H.
	10th		Work as above. Six casualties (1 died of wounds, 3 wounded, 2 shell shock)	N.H.
	11th		Work as above except "D" Coy rested. One casualty (killed)	N.H.
	12		"A" & "B" Coys worked on C.Ts in GUÉMAPPE area. "C" Coy worked on TILLOY - WANCOURT road. "D" Coy worked on CORPS LINE in WANCOURT area. One casualty (wounded)	N.H.
	13th		Work as above. No casualties	N.H.
	14th		Work as above except "B" Coy rested owing to relief. Six casualties (wounded). Reinforcements 4 O.Rs.	N.H.

WAR DIARY
INTELLIGENCE SUMMARY

Army Form C. 2118.

Place	Date 1917	Hour	Summary of Events and Information	Remarks and references to Appendices
TELEGRAPH HILL	May 15		"B" Coy dug C.T in WANCOURT - GUEMAPPE area. "C" Coy worked on TILLOY- WANCOURT road. "A" & "D" Coys rested. Four casualties (Major L.S. Mitchell & Lt-P.H. & Pye-Smith killed. II Lt G & M Thomson wounded. 1 OR Shell shock).	N. 74
	16		"B" & "C" Coy worked on C.Ts in WANCOURT-GUEMAPPE area. "C" Coy supervised infantry working on TILLOY-WANCOURT road. "D" Coy worked on Corps line in WANCOURT area. "A" Coy rested. ("C" Coy relieved "A" Coy). No casualties.	N. 74
	17		"D" Coy relieved "B" Coy. "A" Coy worked on TILLOY-WANCOURT road. "B" Coy worked on Corps line in WANCOURT area "C" & "D" Coys worked on C.T.s in WANCOURT - GUEMAPPE area. 7 Casualties (1 killed, 5 wounded, 1 shell shock).	N. 74
	18		Work as above. No casualties	N. 74
	19		Work as above. No casualties	N. 74
	20		Work as above. No casualties	N. 77
	21		Work as above. One casualty (wounded) Reinforcements 5 O.Rs.	N. 77
	22		Work as above. No casualties	N. 77
	23		Work as above. No casualties	N. 77
	24		Work as above. No casualties (Capt A.F. Trotter, Capt G.J Harris, Lieut & QM. H. Callaghan, II/Lt R.J Chadwick, & R.S.M. C.H. Ginsbury mentioned in Despatches.	N. 77
	25		Work as above. No casualties	N. 77
	26		Work as above. One casualty (wounded)	N. 77
	27		Work as above. No casualties	N. 77
	28		Work as above. Ten casualties (2 killed & wounded). Capt H.R Bennett rejoined. 2 Officers and 20 O.Rs reinforcement. (II/Lt F Rothfield & II/Lt J Williams)	N. 77
	29		Work as above. No casualties. Lt-Col J.E. Ogle mentioned in despatches. "A" Coy relieved "C" Coy. "B" Coy relieved "D" Coy. "A" Coy worked on C.T in WANCOURT- GUEMAPPE area. "B" Coy worked trench boards. "C" Coy worked on TILLOY-WANCOURT road.	N. 77
	30		"D" Coy rested. No casualties (N° 12205 Sgt Munro F & N° 12374 P. S M. Quiggan E. awarded Military Medal.	N. 77

Army Form C. 2118.

WAR DIARY

(Erase heading not required.)

Instructions regarding War Diaries and Intelligence Summaries are contained in F. S. Regs., Part II. and the Staff Manual respectively. Title pages will be prepared in manuscript.

Place	Date	Hour	Summary of Events and Information	Remarks and references to Appendices
TELEGRAPH HILL	May 1917 31st		"A" & "B" Coys worked on C.T. in WANCOURT - GUEMAPPE area. "C" Coy worked on TILLOY - WANCOURT road. "D" Coy on Corps line in WANCOURT area. No casualties.	W. H.

CONFIDENTIAL.

24.Y.
5 sheets

WAR DIARY OF

11TH. (S) BN. THE KING'S. (LIVERPOOL) REGT. (PIONEERS)

FROM 1ST. JUNE 1917.
TO 30TH. JUNE 1917

(VOLUME XXIV).

CONFIDENTIAL

CONFIDENTIAL

14th DIVISION

> 11th BATTALION,
> THE KING'S LIVERPOOL
> REGIMENT (PIONEERS).
> No. C.629/a
> Date 1-7-17

I herewith forward War Diary for the Battalion under my Command from 1st June 1917 to 30th June 1917 (Volume XXIV).

Please acknowledge Receipt.

1/7/17

for Major
Lieut.-Colonel
Commdg. 11th (S) Bn. King's Liverpool Regt. (Pioneers)

WAR DIARY

INTELLIGENCE SUMMARY

Army Form C. 2118.

Place	Date 1917	Hour	Summary of Events and Information	Remarks and references to Appendices
TELEGRAPH HILL	June 1st		"A" & "B" Coys worked on C.T.'s and approaches in WANCOURT-GUEMAPPE area. "C" Coy worked on TILLOY-WANCOURT and roads in WANCOURT-HENINEL area. "D" Coy worked on Corps Line in WANCOURT area. Two casualties (shell shock)	N.N.
	2nd		Work as above. No casualties	N.N.
	3rd		Work as above. One casualty (wounded)	N.N.
	4th		Work as above. No casualties. Lt. Col. P.C. Ogle awarded D.S.O.	N.N.
	5th		Work as above. No casualties. Capt. J.B. Long awarded M.C.	N.N.
	6th		Work as above.	N.N.
NEUVILLE VITASSE	7th		Bn. H.Q. moved to NEUVILLE VITASSE. "A", "B" & "D" Coys worked on C.T.'s & support trenches in WANCOURT-GUEMAPPE area. "C" Coy worked on TILLOY-WANCOURT road and roads in WANCOURT-HENINEL area. No casualties.	N.N.
	8th		The 4 Companies joined Bn. H.Qrs at NEUVILLE VITASSE. Work as yesterday. No casualties	N-N.
	9th		All companies worked on new C.T. from ALBATROSS forward. (N°12390 Sgt T Anderson, N°12872 Sgt T Newell, N°12872 Pte J Nuttall, N°12461 Pte L Brown, & N°21341 Pte T Bonercoft - awarded M.M.)	N.N.
	10th		Work as yesterday. One casualty (wounded)	N.N.
	11th		The Battalion moved to AGNY.	N.N.
	12th		" into billets at BEAUMETZ.	N.N.
	13th		" from BEAUMETZ into billets at SAULTY.	N.N.
ST. LEGER-L-AUTHIE	14th		" SAULTY into billets at ST. LEGER-L-AUTHIE	N.N.
	15th		" rested. Coys were inspected by Coy Officers	N.N.
	16th		" C.O.'s inspection	N.N.

WAR DIARY
INTELLIGENCE SUMMARY

Army Form C.-2118.

Place	Date	Hour	Summary of Events and Information	Remarks and references to Appendices
ST. LEGER L-AUTHIE	June 1917 17th		The Battalion rested in billets. Church Parade.	N.H.
	18th		Training commenced. 7-0 a.m to 7-30 a.m Physical training. 9-0 a.m to 9-45 a.m Platoon Drill. 10-0 to 10-30 a.m. Musketry. 11-0 to 12-0 noon Section Drill. Specialists ie Bombers, Lewis Gunners, and Signallers carried out training under Coy Specialist Officers. 2 to 4 p.m. Games. Reinforcements G.O.Rs	N. H.
	19th		Training continued. Lewis Gunners of "B" "C" & "D" Coys fired grouping practice on 50 yds range.	N.H.
	20th		Training continued. Lewis Gunners of "A" & "B" fired on range.	N.H.
	21st		Training continued. Reinforcements 5. O.Rs	N.H.
	22nd		Training continued. Lewis Gunners of "A" & "B" fired on range.	N.H.
	23rd		Training continued.	N.H.
	24th		Training continued. Musketry :- The Battalion fired grouping practice. Reinforcement 1 O.R.	N.H.
	25th		Training continued. Lewis Gunners of "C" & "D" Coys fired on range.	N.H.
	26th		Divisional Horse Show held at MARIEUX. Reinforcements G.O.Rs	N.H.
	27th		Training continued	N.H.
	28th		The Battalion marched to SAULTY and entrained there for BAILLEUL. Detrained at BAILLEUL and went into camp near LOCRE. Attached to IX Corps CAPT. E.D. LINDOW. R.A.M.C. joined vice LT BOOTHROYD transferred	N.H.
LOCRE	29th		The Battalion rested in camp.	N.H.
	30		The Battalion moved forward to dugouts near KEMMEL	N.H.

CONFIDENTIAL

Vol 25

25 Y.
(4 sheets)

WAR DIARY

OF

11th Bn. "The Kings" (Liverpool) Regt. (Pioneers)

From :- 1st July 1917.
To. :- 31st July. 1917.

(Volume XXV)

WAR DIARY

INTELLIGENCE SUMMARY

Army Form C. 2118.

Place	Date	Hour	Summary of Events and Information	Remarks and references to Appendices
KEMMEL	1917 July 1st		"A" & "B" Coys worked on OOSTAVERNE WOOD tramway line N. of WYTSCHAETE "C" & "D" Coys worked on L'ENFER WOOD tramway line N.W. of MESSINES. No casualties	W.W.
	2nd		Work as above. No casualties	W.W.
	3rd		Work as above. Reinforcements 38.O.Rs	W.W.
	4th		Work as above. No casualties	W.W.
	5th		Work as above. 2 Casualties (wounded) Reinforcements 3. O.Rs	W.W.
	5th		Work as above. No casualties	W.W.
	6th		Work as above. No casualties	W.W.
	7th		Work as above. Lt. g. H. Hopkins rejoined from hospital.	W.W.
	8th		Work as above. No casualties	W.W.
	9th		Work as above. No casualties	W.W.
	10th		Work as above. No casualties	W.W.
	11th		Work as above. One casualty (wounded) II Lt R.Blott transferred to R.F.C & struck off strength	W.W.
			COMPLIMENTARY ORDER received from VII Corps. The Corps Commander is unable to let the 14th (Light) Division leave the Corps without recording his appreciation of the way the 14th Division fought and endured, not only with the main fighting was in progress but also during the very long time the Division was in the line; during the heavy fighting in April and May the Division gallantly carried on the traditions of the light Division of Peninsular fame. He wishes the Division the best of luck, and is certain that wherever it goes it will add to its previous grand record.	
	12th		"A" & "B" Coy worked on OOSTAVERNE WOOD tramway line N. of WYTSCHAETE. "C" & "D" " L'ENFER WOOD tramway line N.W. of MESSINES. No casualties	W.W.
	13th		Work as above. 1 Officer (Capt A.F. Trotter) to UK sick. Struck off strength.	W.W.

WAR DIARY
or
INTELLIGENCE SUMMARY.
(Erase heading not required.)

Army Form C. 2118.

Place	Date	Hour	Summary of Events and Information	Remarks and references to Appendices
KEMMEL	July 1917 14		"A" & "B" Coys worked on OOSTAVERNE WOOD tramway line N of WYTSCHAETE	W.H.
	15		"C" & "D" - " L'ENFER WOOD tramway line N.W. of MESSINES. No casualties	W.H.
			Work as above.	W.H.
	16		"C" & "D" Coys worked on OOSTAVERNE WOOD tramway line, and L'ENFER WOOD line.	W.H.
	17		"A" & "B" - " RIDGE DEFENCES (fire trench) near WYTSCHAETE. No casualties	W.H.
			Work as above. 4 Casualties (wounded)	W.H.
	18		"A" "B" "C" & "D" Worked on RIDGE DEFENCES (trenches) near WYTSCHAETE.	W.H.
			2 Casualties (1 Officer 1 LT T.W. HARDMAN & 1 - OR killed)	W.H.
	19		Work as above (No casualties)	W.H.
	20		Work as above. No casualties (Reinforcements 4 - ORs.)	W.H.
	21		Work as above. 5 Casualties (4 killed 1-wounded)	W.H.
	22		Work as above. No casualties	W.H.
	23		Work as above. No casualties	W.H.
	24		Work as above. No casualties. Reinforcements	W.H.
	25		Work as above. 1 Offr. 6 - ORs. (Capt P.R.F. Mason)	W.H.
	25		Work as above. No casualties	W.H.
	26		Work as above. No casualties	W.H.
	27		Work as above. No casualties	W.H.
	28		Work as above. No casualties	W.H.
	29		Work as above. 2 Casualties (gassed)	W.H.
	30		Work on RIDGE DEFENCES ceased. Battalion standing by for orders. No casualties	W.H.
	31		Battalion stood by for orders. No casualties	W.H.

CONFIDENTIAL

WAR DIARY

OF

11th (S) Bn. The King's Liverpool Regt. (Pioneers)

FROM 1st August 1917

To 31st August 1917.

(VOLUME XXVI)

CONFIDENTIAL

14th (Light) Division

I herewith forward War Diary of the Battn under my Command, from 1st August to 31st August 1917. (Vol. XXVI)

Please acknowledge receipt.

1.9.17

E.C. Ogle
Lieut.-Colonel
Commdg. 11th (S) Bn. King's L'pool Regt. (Pioneers).

11th BATTALION, THE KING'S LIVERPOOL REGIMENT (PIONEERS).
No. S.868
Date 1.9.17

WAR DIARY or INTELLIGENCE SUMMARY

Army Form C. 2118.

Place	Date 1917	Hour	Summary of Events and Information	Remarks and references to Appendices
KEMMEL	Aug 1st		The Battalion stood by for orders. No casualties	N.N.
	2nd		Ditto. No casualties	N.N.
	3rd		Ditto. No casualties	N.N.
	4th		1 Platoon from each Company repaired the Corps Defence Line on the WYTSCHAETE – MESSINES ridge. Reinforcements 4 O.Rs. No casualties	N.N.
	5th		The Battalion stood by for orders. No casualties	N.N.
N.E. of HAZEBROUCK	6th		The Battalion marched into camp, about 2 kilometres N.E. of HAZEBROUCK. No casualties	N.N.
	7th		The Battalion rested in camp. No casualties	N.N.
	8th		The Battalion marched to DICKEBUSCH and took over camp from 23rd Dvl Pioneers. No casualties	N.N.
DICKEBUSCH	9th		All companies making bivouacs and increasing accommodation. No casualties	N.N.
	10th		Roads on which the Battalion will work were reconnoitred. No casualties	N.N.
	11th		"A" Coy. maintenance work on wooden road. "B" Coy. making new wooden road, both near VERBRANDENMOLEN. No casualties	N.N.
	12		"D" Coy relieved "A" Coy, & "C" Coy relieved "B" Coy on above work. No casualties	N.N.
	13		"A" " " "D" " " "B" " " "C" " " . 6 Casualties	N.N.
	14		"D" " " "A" Coy & "C" " " "B" (2 killed 4 wounded). No casualties	N.N.
	15		"A" " " "D" Coy & "B" " " "C" Coy on above work. No casualties, then transport to Hosp. Died	Died
	16th		Battalion rested in bivouacs. No casualties	Died
	17th		Battalion remained in Corps area. Reserve. No casualties	Died

WAR DIARY or INTELLIGENCE SUMMARY.

Army Form C. 2118.

Place	Date	Hour	Summary of Events and Information	Remarks and references to Appendices
28.I.33.b	18th		The Battalion moved from DICKEBUSCH to 28.I.23.b	Ubl
"	19th		O. Coy carried out MENIN Rd in trips. B. Coy on trench from ZILLEBEKE to 28 I.10.d.00	
"			C " " Rd from ZILLEBEKE - BECELAERE RIDGE. 10mm-7 by ol.RE/mlt	Ubl
"			Remainder rested. No casualties	Ubl
"	20th		At 12.45 am men wounded 6 OR below in strength	Ubl
"	21st		At 10.20 pm 4 men slightly wounded at duty 2 OR killed one OR died of wounds. 8 wounded	Ubl
"			3 O.Rs not well, sent to hospital	
"	22nd		The Battalion took to Avenue for Screens for trenches	Ubl
"			On GLENCOURSE WOOD. No casualties	Ubl
"	23rd		Do. do. Do. do. No casualties reported	Ubl
"	24th		The Battalion was to/by for counter attack or GLENCOURSE WOOD but were	Ubl
"			not needed. 200 men helped to evacuate wounded from HOOGE Capt	Ubl
"			F.E. LONG. M.C. killed at HOOGE Capt Bremner the O/C Coy.	Ubl
"	25th		Battalion relieved in trenches & sent 50 OR for carrying wounded Ser	Ubl
"			down from HOOGE. No casualties	
	26		The Battalion moved to WIPPENHOEK area near ABEELE. No casualties	N.N.
	27		" " rested in camp. Reinforcements 5 O.Rs. No casualties	N.N.

Army Form C. 2118.

WAR DIARY
INTELLIGENCE SUMMARY
(Erase heading not required.)

Place	Date	Hour	Summary of Events and Information	Remarks and references to Appendices
near ABEELE	Aug 28 1917		The Battalion rested in camp. No casualties	A-37
	29		" " moved to THIEUSHOUK area. (27W5a 30.50) No casualties	N-37
THIEUSHOUK	30		" " rested in camp. No casualties	A-37
			COMPLIMENTARY ORDER received from Fifth Army.	
			"The Army Commander wishes to thank all ranks 14th (Light) Division for gallant work they have done while with Fifth Army. Despite difficulties of ground, bad weather, and determined resistance of enemy, they made valuable progress along ridge on 22nd August, and maintained position in face of heavy shell fire and repeated counter attacks, inflicting heavy losses. Division has maintained high reputation in some of heaviest fighting on this front."	
	31		Companies carried out training under Coy Officers. No casualties. Reinforcements 7. O.Rs!	N.W.

CONFIDENTIAL

Vol 27

27.Y
5 sheets

WAR DIARY.

OF.

11TH. BN. "THE. KING'S" (LIVERPOOL) REGT. (PIONEERS)

FROM:- 1st SEPTEMBER. 1917.

TO:- 30TH. SEPTEMBER. 1917.

(VOLUME XXVII).

Army Form C. 2118.

WAR DIARY
or
INTELLIGENCE SUMMARY.
(Erase heading not required.)

Instructions regarding War Diaries and Intelligence Summaries are contained in F. S. Regs., Part II. and the Staff Manual respectively. Title pages will be prepared in manuscript.

Place	Date Sept 1917	Hour	Summary of Events and Information	Remarks and references to Appendices
THIEUSHOUK	1		Companies carried out training under Coy Officers. No casualties	N.Th
NEUVE EGLISE	2		The Battalion moved to NEUVE EGLISE (Billets) (1 Cas. E.C. OGLE D.S.O. proceeded to England for duty). No casualties	N.Th
	3		The Battalion remained in billets. Coy Officers reconnoitered work. No casualties	N.Th
WULVERGHEM	4		"A" & "C" Coy worked on FANNY ST communication trench, B & "D" Coys on NEW CROSS communication trenches. "D" Coy also erected screen WULVERGHEM - MESSINES road. All in MESSINES area. No casualties	N.Th
			The Battalion moved into dugouts near WULVERGHEM. Transport remained at NEUVE-EGLISE. 8 Casualties (6 gassed, 2 wounded)	N.Th
	5th		Work as above. 2Lt. S.C. Davey takes over duties of Div. Tramways Officer. 2Lt. L.O. Atkinson rejoined from hospital	N.Th
	6th		Work as above. 2 Casualties (wounded)	
	7th		Work as above. Small party on trench tramways. No casualties. Reinforcements. 2 Officers (2Lt. H.T. CHURCHILL & 2Lt. G. PETRIE)	N.Th
	8th		"A" "B" & "D" Coys. Work as above. "C" Coy laying trench tramway near MESSINES. 2 Casualties (wounded) "Detachment taken from B & Dugouts for 311th Bde R.F.A.	N.Th
	9th		Work as above. 1 Casualty (wounded)	N.Th
	10th		Work as above. 1 Casualty (wounded)	N.Th
	11th		Work as above. No casualties	N.Th
	12		Work as above. 1 Casualty (wounded)	N.Th
	13		Work as above. 5 Casualties (1 Officer 2Lt W. HARRADINE wounded, 4 O.Rs wounded)	N.Th

WAR DIARY or INTELLIGENCE SUMMARY

Army Form C. 2118.

Place	Date	Hour	Summary of Events and Information	Remarks and references to Appendices
WULVERGHEM	Sepr 1917 14th		"A" Coy worked on FANNY ST communication trench. "B" & "D" Coys worked on NEW CROSS communication trench. "D" Coy also erected screen on WULVERGHEM - MESSINES road. "C" Coy laying new switch line or trench tramway. Detachment "C" Coy making gun pits and dugouts for 311th Bde R.F.A. All in MESSINES area. No casualties	T.N. T.N.
	15th		Work as above. "C" Coy also worked on FANNY ST. 1 Casualty (wounded)	T.N. T.N.
	16th		Work as above " " " 2 Casualties (wounded)	T.N. T.N.
	17th		Work as above " " " Reinforcements 4 O.Rs.	T.N. T.N.
	18th		Work as above " " No casualties	T.N. T.N.
	19th		Work as above " " 3 Casualties (wounded)	T.N. T.N.
	20th		Work as above " " No casualties	T.N. T.N.
			2 Casualties (1 wounded, 1 gassed) Reinforcements 1 Officer 1Lt. T.W. WHEELER, 5 O.Rs.	T.N.
	21		Work as above. Detachment "C" Coy returns from 311th Bde R.F.A. No casualties	T.N. T.N.
	22		Work as above. No casualties	T.N. T.N.
	23		Work as above. No casualties	T.N. T.N.
	24		Work as above. No casualties	T.N. T.N.
	25		Work as above. "C" Coy also commenced new Reserve Line E of MESSINES. No casualties	T.N. T.N.
	26		Work as yesterday. 4 Casualties (wounded)	T.N. T.N.
	27		Work as yesterday. No casualties Reinforcement 3 O.Rs	T.N. T.N.

Army Form C. 2118.

WAR DIARY
or
INTELLIGENCE SUMMARY.
(Erase heading not required.)

Place	Date	Hour	Summary of Events and Information	Remarks and references to Appendices
WULVERGHEM	Sept 1917 28		"A" Coy worked on FANNY ST communication trench, "B" & "D" Coy worked on NEW CROSS AV. communication trench. "D" Coy also erected screen on WULVERGHEM — MESSINES road. "C" Coy worked on new Reserve Line. Party from "C" Coy on Trench tramway. No casualties	N.I.N.-
"	29		As above. Enemy shelled 2 Avenue trench. Serjeant Gallagher & 9 men killed	Wd
"	30		As above. No casualties	

CONFIDENTIAL.

WAR DIARY

OF.

11TH. BN. "THE KING'S" (LIVERPOOL) REGT. (PIONEERS)

FROM. 1st. October 1917
TO. 31st. October 1917.

VOLUME XXVIII

Army Form C. 2118.

WAR DIARY
or
INTELLIGENCE SUMMARY.
(Erase heading not required.)

Place	Date	Hour	Summary of Events and Information	Remarks and references to Appendices
WULVERGHEM	1st	-	The Battalion has employed as follows. Running 14th Division Workshops. "A" Coy working on F.M.W.P. Av. "B" Coy working on NEW CROSS ST. E of Reserve Line. "C" Coy " " " RESERVE LINE. "D" Coy " " " W. End of NEW CROSS ST. "C" Coy were also running the Divisional Thine tanning Lyst "D" Coy were no pain with the tramway of LA DOUVE R. from front line to La Petite DOUVE Fm. Of pwrer. Ran Charcoal burning establishment. By workshops, Lyndles pumps. Of pwrer - NEUVE EGLISE Divisional Baths + P8 dumps. Staff arrived 15th OR 454th in strength.	Nil
"	2nd	-	No Casualties.	9.0.
"	3rd	-	As above. No Casualties.	9.0.
"	4th	-	As above. Casualties - 4 O.R. Killed, #8 Wounded - 6 Hospital - 2 wd - 6 duty	9.0.
"	5th	-	No Companies went out to work - Bn warned to stand to for a move - no Casualties	9.0.
"	6	-	B Coy maintaining work as above - Batts less 13 Coy moved to 28/M.17. C.3.9. no Casualties (except 13th reinforcement) NEAR LOCRE	9.0.

WAR DIARY
or
INTELLIGENCE SUMMARY.
(Erase heading not required.)

Army Form C. 2118.

Place	Date	Hour	Summary of Events and Information	Remarks and references to Appendices
M.19.c.3.9 near road	Oct 7		B.Coy. Continuing work on Fanny; Avenue, New Cuts Street, Reserve Line + 14 Que Read Haulways. Bally sers B Coy move to J28.J.19.d.3.0 } MERAUCHN-AREA - no casualties.	ap.
J.19.a.3.0 DICKEBUSCH AREA	8		B.Coy. as above. 150 O.R. left Battalion for 1st R. 26. Kings " authority D.A.G. Base 3/3027-7/7/17 } A.C. & D. Coys. Loaning Lorries with slabs @ R. 2. b4.98, embarking @ Pior Cur Tramway and Constructing road formation from 28-J.14.a.2.6. (Glencorse Wood) [28.I.7.b.39 Casualties 1 man killed - 8 men wounded (Evacuated) 1 wounded - 5 duty	ap.
"	9		A.C. & D. Coys. work as above. B.Coy. moved from 28/T.b.c.1.5 (WULVERGHEM) to the area - 28/I.19.a.3.0. - Casualties, 1 man wounded.	ap.
"	10		Work - as above. - no casualties	ap.
"	11		Following work taken over from 5th Division Pioneer Bn :- Bedford House in 28/I.26. Making up and Clearing old Blaten trench Menin Road :- making good Menin Road for Wagon track - Shrape crab & Claplan line Trench Bd Track "E" 28/I.14.c. Cent. - INVERNESS Copse - T.15.c.05 " " " " "G" - 28/I.19.a.Cent - T.20.7.7.6 - No. Casualties.	ap.
"	12		Work as above. Casualties, 1 man killed.	ap.
"	13		- do - Casualties. O.R. 1 Killed. 2 wounded	ap.

Army Form C. 2118.

WAR DIARY
or
INTELLIGENCE SUMMARY.
(Erase heading not required.)

Instructions regarding War Diaries and Intelligence Summaries are contained in F.S. Regs., Part II. and the Staff Manual respectively. Title pages will be prepared in manuscript.

Place	Date	Hour	Summary of Events and Information	Remarks and references to Appendices
28/ T.19.d.3.0 Luckland area	1917 19/1/17		A & B. Coys. — Work on "Tent Track" from S.K. in 28/J.14.c.2.7. & Fitzclarence Farm — Lone Horse — Tent Street.	
			C. Coy — Work on Track "E" 28/I.24.c. Anhac — N side of Inverness Copse — S. T.14.a.9.3.	G.P.
			D. Coy — Work on Kennis Road diversion & Menin Road from I.18.6.7. & Chateau drive about T.13.a.30.35. — No Casualties. Jigsaw Switch	G.P.
	15.		Work as above. — No Casualties	G.P.
	16.		— do — 1. rank & file 1 wounded	G.P.
	17.		— do — 1. Man wounded	G.P.
	18.		— do — Capt A.C.N. Benny — gassed (P) 4 O.R. wounded, 1 O.R. wounded — off duty	G.P.
	19.		— do — No Casualties	G.P.
	20.		— do — 1. O.R. wounded and 1 wounded — (off duty)	G.P.
	21.		— do — No Casualties	G.P.
	22.		Battalion rested in bivouacs — No Casualties	G.P.
	23.		Maintenance of work detailed above — 1 wounded — (body)	G.P.
	24.		Battalion rested in Bivouacs. — No Casualties	G.P.

Army Form C. 2118.

WAR DIARY
or
INTELLIGENCE SUMMARY.
(Erase heading not required.)

Place	Date	Hour	Summary of Events and Information	Remarks and references to Appendices
28/I.19.d.30	1917 Oct			
PICKEHOUSE AREA	25		A.Coy. Plumer's Drive South in 28/I.24 making formation for plank road. B.C. & D.Coys. making good Menin Road from Jackdaw Fosse to Plumer Drive North in 28.J.13. Casualties:- 1.O.R. wounded. 1 O.R. wounded (at duty)	M.
	26		Battalion rested in Bivouacs – no casualties.	N.
	27		Do do – Casualties – 3.O.R. wounded.	W.
	28		do – 2.O.R. " A Coy camping for 61st Fd.Coy. R.E.	PP.
	29		do – " do	PP.
	30		Battalion rested in Bivouacs – no Casualties	PP.
	31		" carried slab to Plumer Drive for 61st Coy R.E. No casualties	PP.

CONFIDENTIAL.

WAR DIARY

OF

11th (S) Batt? KING'S (L'POOL) REGT (PIONEERS)

FROM   1st November 1917
TO   30th November 1917

(VOLUME XXIX.)

14th Divn

> 11th BATTALION
> THE KING'S LIVERPOOL
> REGIMENT (PIONEERS)
> No. D365/a
> Date 1-12-17

Herewith War Diary of the Battalion under my comd. for the month of November 1917. (Vol XXIX).

Please acknowledge receipt.

1-12-17

S. Bingham Lieut.-Colo.
Commdg. 11th (S) Bn. King's L'pool Regt. (Pioneers)

Army Form C. 2118.

WAR DIARY
or
INTELLIGENCE SUMMARY.
(Erase heading not required.)

Instructions regarding War Diaries and Intelligence Summaries are contained in F. S. Regs., Part II. and the Staff Manual respectively. Title pages will be prepared in manuscript.

Place	Date 1917	Hour	Summary of Events and Information	Remarks and references to Appendices
28/I.19.d.3.0 Buckbush Area	Nov. 1		Battalion resting in Bivouac — reorganisation — no casualties —	App.
	2		do — party of 1 Off and 64 O.R. digging pipeline trench from 28/I.26.0.55.65 to I.26.a.40.95 — no casualties	App.
	3		do do I.26.a.95.27 — no casualties	
			Following "Appreciation" received from X. Corps: "II Corps Commander wishes to express his appreciation of the work done by the Royal Engineers, Pioneer Battalion and Infantry of the 14th Division on the Menin Road and Plumer's Drive despite the appalling conditions, the work of completing Plumer's Drive, and opening up the Menin Road from Hooge has been very rapidly done. He spoke to Plumer's Drive, carried out on the night of 30/31 October, neglects great credit on those concerned." (Sgd) A.R. Cameron, Brig General, General Staff, X. Corps. Noted 31.10.17	App.
	4		Battalion rested in Bivouac. Party of 1 Officer & 64 O.R. digging pipeline trench from I.26.a.95.07 & I.27.a.50.15. no casualties	App.
	5		do Battalion under orders to move to Berthen — no casualties	}App.
	6		Battalion marched to Kieuloux (Berthen area) no casualties	App.

Army Form C. 2118.

WAR DIARY
INTELLIGENCE SUMMARY.
(Erase heading not required.)

Instructions regarding War Diaries and Intelligence Summaries are contained in F. S. Regs., Part II. and the Staff Manual respectively. Title pages will be prepared in manuscript.

Place	Date 1917	Hour	Summary of Events and Information	Remarks and references to Appendices
Husichbrock 27/Q.35. b 1,3	Nov 7		Battalion rested in Billets – no casualties	app
	8		do do do	app
	9		do do under orders to move to Wamantinghe area	app
Wamantinghe Area	10		do moved to Wamantinghe area – no casualties	app
28.H.16.a	11		do rested in tents. The Comm'd'g Officer held a Conference with O.C. Coys at which details of work were arranged re carrying for and constructing corduroy track under Abraham Heights. – no casualties	app
Potijze Area 28.I.3.d	12		A & B. Coys moved to 28.I.3.d and commenced work same night as under:–	
	12/13		WORK. A.Coy. Carrg slabs and sandbags, felling logs and preparing forrain 28/D.14.a.3.1 to 28/D.14.3.44	app
			B.Coy. –do– and repairing and maintaining road from Spree Farm 28/C.18.d. to Roadend at about 28/D.15.b. Central. – no casualties	app
	13		H.Q., C + D. Coys moved to 28/I.3.d. – C & D. Coys commenced work same night as under:–	
	13/14		WORK. C. Coy. Packing corduroy road from 28/D.15.b.5.1. to 28/D.15.a.95.65. and carryg slabs on to work	app
			D. Coy. Carrg, pil'g, loading & unloading trucks for slab work in 28/D.9.a. – No casualties	app

1577 Wt.W10791/1773 500,000 1/15 D.D.&L. A.D.S.S./Forms/C. 2118.

Army Form C. 2118.

WAR DIARY
or
INTELLIGENCE SUMMARY.
(Erase heading not required.)

Place	Date 1917	Hour	Summary of Events and Information	Remarks and references to Appendices
POTIJZE AREA 28/I.3.d	Nov 13/14		A. Coy. Continued work as for the 13th. B. Coy. Repair maintenance of road between Spree Farm 28/C.18.a and Kansas Cross 28/D.14.a. No casualties	WP
	14/15		A. Coy — continued work as above. B. Coy — work as above. C. Coy — do do as for 14th. D. Coy — work as for 14th. No casualties	WP
	15/16		A. Coy do do 15th. B. Coy — work as above. C. " Double tracking Cooway Road from 28/D.a.8.8 to D.15.7.00.75. D. " Carrying plank standings - felling slaying logs - levelling cult pits - Brienen ap road - Saalystraas X Road. NO CASUALTIES	W
	16/17		A, B, C & D Coys. work as for 15/16. 1.O.R slightly wounded (remain at duty)	W
	17/18		A & B Coy. work as per 16/17. C. Coy. Double tracking road D.15.7.00.75 to Bridgette C.24.9. D. Coy. Ekerlies totalling road — 3 relays — to Potampteyale D.16.2.25.60. Casualties 1.O.R killed D.13.?	WP
	18/19		Work as above — continued from 18th. No Casualties	WP

1577 Wt.W10791/1773 500,000 1/15 D.D. & L. A.D.S.S./Forms/C. 2118.

Army Form C. 2118.

WAR DIARY
or
INTELLIGENCE SUMMARY.
(Erase heading not required.)

Instructions regarding War Diaries and Intelligence
Summaries are contained in F. S. Regs., Part II.
and the Staff Manual respectively. Title pages
will be prepared in manuscript.

Place	Date	Hour	Summary of Events and Information	Remarks and references to Appendices
POTIJZE AREA 28/I.3.d.	1917 Nov 20		Work on Corduroy Road as per Appendix A. - Hydration of Coys	Ap.
	21		do Casualties nil	Ap.
	22		do Casualties nil	Ap.
	23		do Casualties nil	Ap.
	24		do Casualties nil 2. O.R. wounded (duty)	Ap.
			The following letter was received from the Canadian Corps Commander - addressed to O/C 11"Bn "H.King's "Liverpool Regiment. Begins - "On handing over command of the PASSCHENDAELE front, I wish to express to you and to the Officers, N.C.O.'s, and men under your command my warm appreciation of the excellent work which they have done for the Canadian Corps while under my command. Their work has had to be carried out under very arduous and trying circumstances, with the stimulus of actually taking part in the offensive themselves, although exposed to heavy shell fire which has, I am sorry to say, at times resulted in considerable casualties. The work that they have done has contributed to the success of the operations in the most direct degree, and it is no exaggeration to say that without such work no offensive could be successfully undertaken." (Signed) A.W.Currie Lieut.General. Comm'g. Canadian Corps.	Ap.
	Major. 30/11			

Army Form C. 2118.

WAR DIARY
INTELLIGENCE SUMMARY.
(Erase heading not required.)

Instructions regarding War Diaries and Intelligence
Summaries are contained in F. S. Regs., Part II.
and the Staff Manual respectively. Title pages
will be prepared in manuscript.

Place	Date 1917	Hour	Summary of Events and Information	Remarks and references to Appendices
POTIJZE AREA 28.I.3.d	Nov 25		Work on Cordray Road Kansas Cross — No attack, vide appendix "A". Maintenance repair. Double tracking. Rating ratings — By rotation of Coys	App
	26		do	App.
	27		do	App.
	28		do M/N 17/8 to 6 AM and 6 p.m. to 6 M/N 28/29 — 1 O.R. killed 28/C.27.a.7.5. East of St. Jean.	App.
ST JEAN AREA 26/C.27.d.9.5.	29		Battalion moved to 3 O.R. wounded	App.
	30		Work as above do 1. O.R. wounded.	App.

WAR DIARY

OF

11TH Battalion KING'S L'POOL REGT (Pioneers)

From December 1st 1917

To December 31st 1917.

(VOL. XXX)

Army Form C. 2118.

WAR DIARY
INTELLIGENCE SUMMARY.
(Erase heading not required.)

Instructions regarding War Diaries and Intelligence
Summaries are contained in F. S. Regs., Part II.
and the Staff Manual respectively. Title pages
will be prepared in manuscript.

Place	Date 1917	Hour	Summary of Events and Information	Remarks and references to Appendices
POTIJZE-STEEN AREA 28.C.7.d.9.5.	Dec 1		WORK Maintenance and repair of Cameron Road from Bridge House 28/C.24.b via Kansas Cross to No 5 track 28/D.15.b. and Northern Spur from 28/D.15.a.0.7 by Rotation of Companies. No Casualties	GP.
	2		Work as above Work handed over to 22nd Durham L.I. 2.O.R. wounded — 1 wounded	GP.
	3		Work taken over from 22nd Durham L.I. — No.5. TRACK Doubletracking & haunch g — Northern Arm. 28/D.9.a.8.4 to 20/V.30. Central do — Southern " ditto to 28/D.6.a.75.60 MULE TRACK (CAD ROAD) Maintce & improvement from Kansas Cross. 28/D.14.a.2.1 to Gravenstafel 28/D.9.c.3.2 Casualties Nil.	GP.
	4		Work as above on Northern Arm only. 2. O.R. wounded	GP.
	5		do Battn carried & more to La Brique — 28/C.26.d.5.0 on 1. Slight casualties (remain on duty) 1. accidentally wounded.	GP.
	6		and on mule track H.Q. A + C Coy moved to 28/C.26.d.5.0	GP.
	7		do do do do	GP.

WAR DIARY
or
INTELLIGENCE SUMMARY.
(Erase heading not required.)

Army Form C. 2118.

Place	Date Dec 1917	Hour	Summary of Events and Information	Remarks and references to Appendices
LaBasque 28/C.26.a.5.0	8		Work :- Maintenance repair of Mule Track from 28/D.9.a.75.35 to Northern Avo. 20/V.30 Central. Maintenance repair of mule track 28/D.15.a.0.7 to Relieve 29/D.4.a. Casualties. 2. O.R. killed	GP
	9		Work as above. Casualties Nil	GP
	10		- do - on the Southern ARM from "Berlin" 29/B.9.a.74 to moselmart 28/B.6.a.5.9 and maintenance + repair of Muletrack as above. 2 Lt T.W. Wheeler wounded - other Casualties - NIL -	GP
	11		Work as above. Casualties Nil	GP
	12		- do - (less Mule Track) and plus - Improvement of shelter and work on Dressing Station 28/C.14.a and 28/B.13.c Casualties NIL	GP
	13		Work as above (ints) Casualties 1.O.R. wounded	GP
	14		Work for 13th less shelter plus MULE TRACK from Kansas Cross to Gravenstafel. Casualties NIL	GP

Army Form C. 2118.

WAR DIARY
or
INTELLIGENCE SUMMARY.
(Erase heading not required.)

Instructions regarding War Diaries and Intelligence Summaries are contained in F.S. Regs., Part II and the Staff Manual respectively. Title pages will be prepared in manuscript.

Place	Date 1917	Hour	Summary of Events and Information	Remarks and references to Appendices
Kafuque 28/C.31.d.5.0	15		WORK. Maintenance and repair of No 5 Track. Southern Arm from Behn - 28/D.9.d.7.4 to 28/D.6.a.5.9. Maintenance and repair between Ransomes & Bellevue. Casualties. Nil.	Ap.
	16		Work as above. Casualties 2/O.R. killed. 5/O.R. wounded (1 since died).	Ap.
	17		- do - Casualties nil.	Ap.
	18		- do - Casualties nil.	Ap.
	19		- do - Casualties. 1. O.R. wounded	Ap.
	20		- do - 2/Lt Caldwell wounded 2.O.R. wounded	Ap.
	21		- do - 1. wounded (at duty)	Ap.
	22		Work on mule track as above - (1. Company) 2. Coys. Employed marking out No 6. Track with screw pickets. Casual(t). Nil.	Ap.

Army Form C. 2118.

WAR DIARY
or
INTELLIGENCE SUMMARY.
(Erase heading not required.)

Instructions regarding War Diaries and Intelligence Summaries are contained in F. S. Regs., Part II. and the Staff Manual respectively. Title pages will be prepared in manuscript.

Place	Date 1917	Hour	Summary of Events and Information	Remarks and references to Appendices
Lasbuque 28.S.d.5.0.	Dec 23		WORK Maintenance repair of No 5 Track and double tracking from "Berlin" - 28/O.9.d.7.4 to Roulecroft 28/O.6.a.5.9. Maintenance and repair of Rail Track 28/O.W.B.9.6 & 28/O.S.C.0.6. Casualties - on work Nil " from Hostile Aircraft. (Bomb dropped on Capt.) 1.OR Killed 2.OR Ond grooms 15.OR Wounded - Capt Stephens had (1 Series died 24/12)	A.P.
	24		Work as above Casualties 1.OR Wounded	H.
	25		work as above Casualties Nil	H.
	26		work as above. Reconnected work on Paniet Road to be taken over from 23.A.L.I. on 27th A Coy proceed to Red via Watou Casualties. 1 wounded (at Arg) 21st Bn. Sent down today	JWD
	27		WORK Maintenance repair & improvement of PANET ROAD from KANSAS CROSS to NORTHERN SPUR Casualties nil.	JWD
	28		work as above Casualties Nil	JWD

Army Form C. 2118.

WAR DIARY
or
INTELLIGENCE SUMMARY.

(Erase heading not required.)

Instructions regarding War Diaries and Intelligence Summaries are contained in F. S. Regs., Part II. and the Staff Manual respectively. Title pages will be prepared in manuscript.

Place	Date 1917	Hour	Summary of Events and Information	Remarks and references to Appendices
LA BRIQUE 28/C.26d5.0.	Dec 29		WORK Maintenance, repair, improvement of PANET ROAD from KANSAS CROSS to NORTHERN SPUR Casualties nil	MJ
	30		Work as above Casualties one	MJ
	31		(B.C. D.E. up) Battalion finished work on PANET ROAD at 5. a.m. A coy left water for ZERMEZEELE Casualties nil Transport proceeded to ZERMEZEELE	MJ

A5834 Wt. W4973/M687 750,000 8/16 D. D. & L. Ltd. Forms/C.2118/13.

WAR DIARY

OF

11th (S.) Battalion KINGS (L'POOL) REGT. (PIONEERS)

From   January 1st. 1918

To   January 31st. 1918.

(VOL XXXI.)

Army Form C. 2118.

WAR DIARY
or
INTELLIGENCE SUMMARY.
(Erase heading not required.)

Instructions regarding War Diaries and Intelligence Summaries are contained in F.S. Regs., Part II. and the Staff Manual respectively. Title pages will be prepared in manuscript.

Place	Date 1918	Hour	Summary of Events and Information	Remarks and references to Appendices
ST MARTIN AU LAERT	1st Jan		Battalion (B.C. & D Coys) entrained at VLAMENTINGHE STATION 2.30/am Advanced at WIZERNES 11.20/am ST MARTIN AU LAERT A Coy reported Battalion at WATTEN ZEELE. No casualties	JWG
"	2nd		Battalion rested in billets. No casualties	JWG
"	3rd		Battalion rested in billets. No casualties	JWG
"	4th		Battalion entrained at St Omer D Coy 2.30 am remainder 5.0 am detrained Edgehill 11.30am " 1.30pm proceeded to Bray (Morlancourt Camp) 2.0pm. no casualties	JWG
BRAY Morlancourt Camp (12 D) R4a3b	5th		Battalion rested in camp. no casualties	{ I.O.R convened 23.12.17 bad ground 5.1.18 } JWG
"	6th		Battalion rested in camp. no casualties	JWG
"	7th		Battalion rested in camp. no casualties	JWG

WAR DIARY
or
INTELLIGENCE SUMMARY.

(Erase heading not required.)

Army Form C. 2118.

Place	Date 1/18	Hour	Summary of Events and Information	Remarks and references to Appendices
MARLEY CAMP 62D / R4 d 2.6	8/1/18		Battalion rested in camp	DWJ
	9/1/18		Draft of 100 O.R. arrived taken on strength no casualties	DWJ
	10/1/18		Battalion rested in camp no casualties	DWJ
			Battalion rested in camp 100 O.R. left for 12th Battalion The Kings' no casualties	DWJ
	11/1/18		Battalion rested in camp. 100 O.R. left for 12 Battalion The Kings no casualties.	DWJ
	12/1/18		Battalion rested in camp no casualties	DWJ
	13/1/18		do do do —	DWJ
	14/1/18		do do —	DWJ
	15/1/18		do do —	DWJ

Army Form C. 2118.

WAR DIARY
or
INTELLIGENCE SUMMARY.
(Erase heading not required.)

Instructions regarding War Diaries and Intelligence Summaries are contained in F. S. Regs., Part II. and the Staff Manual respectively. Title pages will be prepared in manuscript.

Place	Date 1918	Hour	Summary of Events and Information	Remarks and references to Appendices
MARLEY CAMP FRANCE 62.a. R 4.d.3.6	Jan 16		Battalion rested in Camp.	No casualties. App
	17/18		-do-	no casualties App
	18/18		-do-	no casualties App
	19/18		-do-	no casualties App
	20/18		-do- Stand to for a move	no casualties App
	21/18		-do- Prepared for move	do App
Ret Map (i) Amiens	22/18		Battalion marched to Hangest-en-Santere and spent the night in billets.	App no casualties
	23/18		do Rosieres	do App
	24/18		do Dives.	do App
	25/18		do Guiscard	do App
(i) St Quentin	26/18		do rested in billets.	do App
	27/18		"A" Coy moved forward to dugouts at CAPONNE FARM 66c/H.28.d. "B" & "C" Coys moved into Dugouts at LES SAULES 66c/H.14.c. 30 men from "D" Coy proceeded to MONTESCOURT Dump for N. St. working party. H.Qrs & remainder of "D" Coy remained at GUISCARD. No casualties.	App

Army Form C. 2118.

WAR DIARY
or
INTELLIGENCE SUMMARY.

(Erase heading not required.)

Instructions regarding War Diaries and Intelligence Summaries are contained in F. S. Regs., Part II. and the Staff Manual respectively. Title pages will be prepared in manuscript.

Place	Date	Hour	Summary of Events and Information	Remarks and references to Appendices
ST QUENTIN	Jan 28	1918	Bn H.Qrs. & remainder of "D" Coy marched into dugouts at MONTESCOURT. "A" Coy rested. "B" Coy widened & cleared C.T. BOYAU DE FRANCE 66c.B.22.a.5.2. "C" Coy worked on C.T. AMERICA 66c.H.14.&.8.1. "D" Coy. 30 men at MONTESCOURT Dump. No casualties	7N-74.
MONTESCOURT	29		"A" Coy worked on C.T. BOYAU DE VILAINE 66c.I.19.a.52. "B" & "C" Coys as yesterday. Party of 30 men from "D" Coy unloading ammunition. No casualties	7N-74.
	30		"A" Coy as yesterday. "B" Coy worked on BOYAU DE LORRAINE C.T. & BOYAU LA SOMME C.T. "C" Coys as yesterday. "D" Coy. 30 men at MONTESCOURT. & 12 men repairing MONTESCOURT - ESSIGNY road. 66c.H7c.5.4. No casualties	7N 7N.
	31		Work as yesterday Casualties 2 Men gassed.	7N. 7N.

WAR DIARY.

11TH BN KING'S (L'POOL) REGIMENT (PIONEERS)

FROM Feb 1st 1918
TO Feb 28th 1918

(VOLUME XXXII)

Confidential

14th (Light) Divn

[Stamp: 11th BATTALION, THE KING'S LIVERPOOL REGIMENT (PIONEERS). No. D711/a Date 1-3-18]

Herewith War Diary of the Battalion under my Comd for February 1918 (Volume XXXII)

Please acknowledge

1 3/18

H Payne Capt
for Lieut Col
Comdg 11th (S) Bn. King's L'pool Regt. (Pioneers)

Army Form C. 2118.

WAR DIARY
or
INTELLIGENCE SUMMARY.
(Erase heading not required.)

Instructions regarding War Diaries and Intelligence Summaries are contained in F. S. Regs., Part II and the Staff Manual respectively. Title pages will be prepared in manuscript.

Place	Date	Hour	Summary of Events and Information	Remarks and references to Appendices
MONTESCOURT	Feb 1918			
	1		Bn. H.Qrs. + "D" Coy at MONTESCOURT. "A" Coy at CAPONNE FARM 66c/1.19 a 5.2. "B" Coy & "C" Coy at LES SAULES 66/c/.13c.6.2. "B" Coy worked on BOYAU DE VILAINE C.T. 66c/1.13c.6.2. "B" Coy on BOYAU DE LORRAINE + BOYAU LA SOMME C.Ts. "C" Coy on BOYAU AMERIQUE + BOYAU CHICAGO. "D" Coy. 30 men at R.E. Dump MONTESCOURT 20 men unloading at dump and 12 men repairing MONTESCOURT-ESSIGNY Road. No casualties	₣#5
	2		Work as above	₣#5
	3		Work as above	₣#5
	4		Work as yesterday. "D" Coy also commenced work on Rear Defence Line. MONTESCOURT. No casualties	₣#5
	5		Work as yesterday. No casualties	₣#5
	6		Work as yesterday. One man slightly gassed. Draft of 4 officers and 135 other ranks arrived as reinforcements from 2/5 Kings. "D" Coy reconnoitred BOYAU DE FRANCE between LA MANUFACTURE FARM and LE CORNET D'OR and made report of work to be done. also been seen for the defence of right flank.	₣#5
	7		Work as yesterday. No casualties	₣#5
	8		Work as yesterday. "C" Coy also commenced work on two Strong Points at H14.6.5.7 and H15.6.4.3 nr Corps Line. No casualties	₣#5.
	9		Work as yesterday. No casualties	₣#5.
	10		Work as yesterday. "D" Coy also made 2 level crossings. G29.C.75.00 and M11a.70.5.5. Ref. Map. 66c NW 3 & 66c NW III. No casualties	H.H.

WAR DIARY
or
INTELLIGENCE SUMMARY.
(Erase heading not required.)

Army Form C. 2118.

Place	Date Feb	Hour 1918	Summary of Events and Information	Remarks and references to Appendices
MONTESCOURT	11		"A" Coy worked on BOYAU DE VILAINE. C.T. "B" Coy on BOYAU DE LORRAINE and BOYAU LA SOMME. C.Ts. "C" Coy continued work on AMERICA Strong Points. "D" Coy commenced work on 3 Strong Points. 10.O.R's arrived as reinforcement from 2/5 Bn Kings and 2 O.R's from Base.	
	12		Work as above.	No casualties
	13		Work as above.	No casualties
	14		Work as above.	No casualties
	15		Work as above. 1 Lt. O.C. McINTOSH joined from 2/5 Bn.	No Casualties
	16		Work as above. "D" Coy sent 1 platoon to erect and improve dugouts in 66C. H20.	No casualties
	17		Work as above. "C" Coy also worked on BREST. F.T. Map ref 66C. H11d.6.9 to H11d.9.5. "B" on ALSACE C.T.	No casualties
	18		Work as above. "D" Coy also on level crossings.	No casualties
	19		Work as above. "A" Coy also worked on SEINE. C.T.	No casualties
	20		Work as above.	2 casualties (wounded)
	21		Work as above.	1 casualty (1. O.R wounded)
	22		Work as above.	No casualties
	23		Work as above.	No casualties
	24		Work as above.	No casualties
	25		Work as above.	No casualties

Army Form C. 2118.

WAR DIARY
or
INTELLIGENCE SUMMARY.
(Erase heading not required.)

Place	Date	Hour	Summary of Events and Information	Remarks and references to Appendices
MONTESCOURT	Feb 1918 26		"B" Coy worked on FLORRAINE C.T., SOMME C.T., ALSACE C.T., BOYAU DE FRANCE from "D" Coy. "C" Coy worked on AMERICA C.T. and strong points. The re-organization of the Battalion took place. 4th & 3 company of "D" Coy being sent to "A", "B", & "C" Coys as follows. N.º 13 platoon to "A" Coy, N.º 16 platoon to "B" Coy & 15 platoon to "C" Coy. Battalion H.Q.rs moved from MONTESCOURT to LA MOTTE near to CLASTRES. "A" Coy moved 100 men to ESSIGNY KEEP, the remainder of the Coy. into huts at LA MOTTE and CLASTRES. "B" Coy also commenced work on mined dugouts at LA MANUFACTURE FARM. No casualties	W.H.
	27		Work as above. No casualties	W.H.
	28		Work as above. "A" Coy worked on ESSIGNY KEEP. "Battle Zone Take precautionary action" Message of Battalion received at 1-0 p.m. "Stand to arms". Prepared to move at 1 hours notice. Precautionary action was cancelled by wire at 11-30 p.m. A draft of 57 O.R.s arrived at 12-0 noon. No casualties	W.H.

WAR DIARY

11th Bn KING'S LIVERPOOL REGT (Pioneers)

From   March 1st 1918
To   March 31st 1918

(VOLUME XXXIII)

WAR DIARY or INTELLIGENCE SUMMARY.

Army Form C. 2118.

Place	Date	Hour	Summary of Events and Information	Remarks and references to Appendices
CLASTRES	March 1918 1		"B" & "C" Coy in dugouts at LES SAULES 66/c/H14c. 50 men "A" Coy in dugouts near ESSIGNY, N.N. remainder of "A" in huts at CLASTRE. H.Qrs at LA MOTTE FARM near CLASTRE. "A" Coy had 20 men putting in switch lines for Divl Signal Coy & 30 men working on ESSIGNY KEEP. "B" Coy worked on "LORRAINE, ALSACE, SOMME and FRANCE" communication trenches, strengthened cellars in ESSIGNY, and continued work on mined dugout at LA MANUFACTURE FARM. "C" Coy worked on VERDUN and AMERICA C.T's. The Commanding Officer inspected new draft. No casualties	H.H.
66C	2		Work as above. "C" Coy also commenced work on shelters in Battle Zone.	H.H.
	3		"A" Coy commenced work on 41st Bde Battle H.Qrs G24.a.2.1.& 25. O.R's from Draft posted to "C" Coy, and joined them at LES SAULES G30d.1.4. No casualties	H.H.
	4		Work as above	H.H.
	5		Work as above. Major H.N. GILES joined from 2/5 Bn Kings. "B" Coy also worked on II Lt A.H. PALMER admitted to hospital. No casualties	H.H.
			Work as above BENAY KEEP. (66c H21c88) No casualties	H.H.
	6		Work as above No casualties	P.P.
	7		Major H.N. GILES proceeded to take over Area Commandant at BEAUMONT-EN-BEINE relieving II Lt. M. HAWKSWORTH. No casualties	P.P.
	8		Work as above Capt. A CRUNDWELL proceeded to take over the duties of Area Commandant at JUSSY. Reinforcements:- 6 O.R. arrived from "G" Group Base. No casualties	P.P.

Army Form C. 2118.

WAR DIARY
or
INTELLIGENCE SUMMARY.
(Erase heading not required.)

Instructions regarding War Diaries and Intelligence Summaries are contained in F. S. Regs., Part II. and the Staff Manual respectively. Title pages will be prepared in manuscript.

Place	Date March 1918	Hour	Summary of Events and Information	Remarks and references to Appendices
CLASTRES. 6GC.	9.		'B' Coy. commenced to work on 43rd Brigade H.Q. at G.18.d.3.0. (Other work as before.) Summer time came into use at 11 p.m. (Winter time) supper at 11 p.m. clocks were put forward one hour. 2/Lt. M. HAWKSWORTH, late Area Commandant of BEAUMONT-EN-BEINES, rejoined Battn.	no casualties P.P.
	10.		Work as above. Lt. F. J. HORTH, & 2/Lt. R. H. HEAPS attacked for duty to 61st and 62nd Field Coys. R.E. respectively.	P.P.
	11.		Work as above. 'A' Coy. ceased to work on DUGOUT for 41st Bde. Battle H.Q. and commenced work in a shaft G.24.d.4.3.	no casualties P.P. no Casualties. P.P.
	12.		Work as above	no Casualties. P.P.
	13.		Work as above. 'B' Coy. finished working on Dugout at LA MANUFACTURE H.d.1.5. 2/Lt. E. V. HOOKHAM commenced his duties as Divisional Agricultural Officer.	P.P. no Casualties.
	14.		'A' Coy. commenced work on 43 BDE Dugout at G.36.b.4. 'B' Coy began work on 41st/3D DETHQ Dugout at G.29.b.1.1. Remainder of work as usual. Road at LA MOTTE reclaimed by Battn. H.Q.	P.P. no Casualties.
	15.		Work as above.	no Casualties. P.P.
	16.		The following officers were temporarily cross posted with effect from today:— 2/Lt. A. H. PALMER & 2/Lt. BLUNDELL E.A. 2/Lt. KNIGHT W.J. 2/Lt. W. A. ROBBINS 7 M.R.B. 2/Lt. DICKSON R.M. 9 R.B. 2/Lt. ADAMS.F.B. 8 K.R.R.C. 2/Lt. DODDS.J.H. 9 K.R.R.C. 2/Lt. COCKBURN E. & SOMERSET L.I. 2/Lt. WRATTON C.J. 2/Lt. Mc.INTOSH.O. 9 S.R. Work as above	P.P. no Casualties

WAR DIARY
or
INTELLIGENCE SUMMARY.

Army Form C. 2118.

Place	Date March 1918	Hour	Summary of Events and Information	Remarks and references to Appendices
CLASTRES 66.c.	17		Work as above. Major J.H. KEITH, 6th Bn Scottish Rifles, was attached to the Bn for rations and accommodation. No casualties.	N.74.
	18		Work as above. No casualties	N.74.
	19		Work as above. About 11.0 p.m. a wire was received to commence on the night 20/21st reported that the enemy offensive was to commence on the night 20/21st. Orders came later that working parties were to cease and all troops to be ready on the 20th. No casualties.	N.74
	20		Troops rested. Wire received from Div. "BATTLE ZONE TAKE PRECAUTIONARY ACTION." "B" & "C" Coys came under orders of 42nd Bde, and the detachment of "A" Coy under It Lt HORROCKS in dugouts near ESSIGNY came under orders of 41st Bde. "A" Coy and Bn HQrs came into Divisional reserve. No casualties	N.74.
	21		Heavy enemy bombardment commenced at 4-30 a.m. At 5-30 a.m. message received from Division "INFANTRY OCCUPY BATTLE ZONE." Battalion "stood to" and prepared to move at short notice. Terrific bombardment continued all morning, but no news came through. At 1-0 p.m. verbal message from an orderly that the enemy had broken through and was in ESSIGNY. Also that Div HQrs were preparing to evacuate CLASTRES. Orders received from Div. that all transport was to move back to LA NEUVILLE. Runner came through and reported that "B" & "C" Coys were in action and holding strong points near LAMBAY WOOD and BENAY. Orders received at 3-0 p.m. for "A" Coy to move forward and report to 41st Bde HQrs at G.29 central. At 11-0 p.m. orders received from Div. to move back to DETROIT BLEU. "A" Coy rejoined at CLASTRES and moved back to with HQrs to JUSSY when they came again under orders of 41st Bde. Bn H.Qrs billeted at DETROIT BLEU. "B" & "C" Coys moved under 42nd Bde ordered. British line drawn back during night of 21/22nd to S.W. side of CROZAT canal.	N.74

WAR DIARY or INTELLIGENCE SUMMARY

Army Form C. 2118.

Place	Date	Hour	Summary of Events and Information	Remarks and references to Appendices
CLASTRES	March 21 (cont)		Casualties :- 2 Lt J.T. WILLIAMS killed, Capt M.C.M. DENNY wounded. 18 - O.Rs killed. 65 - O.Rs wounded, 8 - O.Rs wounded & missing 78 - O.Rs missing	W.H.
DETROIT BLEU	22		"A" Coy at FLAVY LE MARTEL under 41st Bde. "B" & "C" Coys rested at PETIT DETROIT. At 6-0 pm orders received for Bn. H.Qrs to move to BEAUMONT EN BEINE. Moved at 9-0 p.m. and arrived at destination at 11-0 a.m. The Transport formed at BEAUMONT under orders from 42nd Bde. "A" Coy in action along Railway between JUSSY and FLAVY. Casualties. 5 - O.Rs wounded.	W.H.
BEAUMONT EN BEINE	23		"A", "B", & "C" Coys in action near FLAVY LE MARTEL. About 10 a.m. orders received from Div. for all Transport to move to BEINES. H.Qrs and all available men moved E. of BEAUMONT in reserve. On arrival of Transport at BEINES, they were instructed by Div. to move still further back, and Transport moved to QUESMY. Rested there until evening and then moved into billets at NOYON. Casualties :- Killed { Capt. H.R. BENNETT II Lieut J.J. GRIFFITHS 5 - O.Rs. Wounded { II Lieut J.C. HORROCKS II Lieut T. TELFORD 4½ - O.Rs Wounded & Missing { Capt A. CRUNDWELL 17 - O.Rs. Missing { a/Capt. W.R.A. WAREING Lieut J.E. ACHESON 61 - O.Rs.	W.H.

Army Form C. 2118.

WAR DIARY
or
INTELLIGENCE SUMMARY.
(Erase heading not required.)

Instructions regarding War Diaries and Intelligence Summaries are contained in F. S. Regs., Part II. and the Staff Manual respectively. Title pages will be prepared in manuscript.

Place	Date 1918	Hour	Summary of Events and Information	Remarks and references to Appendices
NOYON	24th March		At 11-30 a.m. message received that the C.O, Adjt., & R.S.M. were to proceed to GUISCARD at once. The C.O to take command of all details of the 42nd Inf. Bde. II Lt. GARNHAM with 20 men of "A" Coy, reported H.Q.rs at NOYON. Capt G.J.HARRIS with 18 men of "C" Coy at GUISCARD with details of 42nd Bde. A composite battalion was formed of all details with the C.O in command. Strength about 500. At 6-30 p.m. the battalion with 42nd Bde. H.Q.rs moved to CRISOLLES, and at 10-0 p.m. moved to SERMAIZE. 3 Patrols were posted on the N.E. side of the dry canal. 50 men in support on the South of the canal. The remainder in reserve in the village. The Reg.t Transport moved from NOYON to DIVES. No casualties	H. F.
SERMAIZE	25		At 8-0 a.m. news that the enemy was approaching was received, and a fire trench was dug on the S.W. side of the canal. The composite battalion manned the trench. At 5-0 p.m. parties of French troops were seen retiring on both flanks, in good order. At 5.15 p.m. the enemy were seen coming over the crest of the ridge on the N side of the canal. Fire was opened and their advance checked for a short time. At 6-50 p.m. we commenced to withdraw. Withdrawal completed successfully. This area was taken over by the French. Marched to THIESCOURT and billeted. No casualties	H. F.
THIESCOURT	26		All details formed into their respective battalions, and marched to high ground S.W of L'ECOUVILLON. Battalion allotted position in reserve. In afternoon, marched to billets in ELINCOURT. Transport moved from DIVES to GIRAUMONT. No casualties	H. F.

War Diary
or
Intelligence Summary.

Army Form C. 2118.

Place	Date hour	Summary of Events and Information	Remarks
ELINCOURT	Mar 27 1918	Bn. marched from ELINCOURT to REMY where transport and details joined. Bivouaced in field. No casualties	H.N.
REMY	28	At 10-0 a.m. Bn "stood to" as situation was still obscure. Left REMY at 6-0 p.m. and marched to billets at FM DE L'EVECHE, near PONT-SUR-MAXENCE. No casualties	H.N.
PONT SUR MAXENCE.	29	At 5-15 p.m. marched to NOGENT to embus for HEBECOURT. S.W. of AMIENS. This order cancelled en route, and Bn marched to CREIL and billeted for night. No casualties	H.N.
CREIL	30	Marched to billets at F.M. SEBASTOPOL near AIRION. No casualties	H.N.
AIRION	31	Moved by march to billets at WAVIGNIES. No casualties	H.N.
		Map references. Sheet 66 C. France. ST.QUENTIN.18. and AMIENS.17.	H.N.

Pioneers.
14th Div.

Battn. was disbanded 27.4.18.

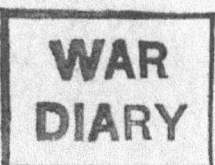

11th BATTN. THE KING'S (LIVERPOOL REGIMENT).

A P R I L

(1/27.4.18)

1 9 1 8

14th DIVN.

> 11th BATTALION,
> THE KING'S LIVERPOOL
> REGIMENT (PIONEERS).
> No. D899/a
> Date. 30-4-18

I herewith forward War Diary for the Battn under my Comd for the month of April 1918 (10cxxxiv)

Please acknowledge receipt

30/4/18

S. Blyth, Lieut Col
Comdg 11th (S) Bn. King's L'pool Regt. (Pioneers)

M.S. Army Form C.2118.

Intelligence Summary.

Summary of Events and Information

Place	Date April 1918	Hour	Summary of Events and Information	Remarks
WAVIGNIES	1st		The Battalion marched from WAVIGNIES to BONNEUIL. No casualties	H.H.
BONNEUIL	2		" " BONNEUIL to ST. SAUFLIEU and then proceeded by bus to BOVES. Transport in wood S. of BOVES. No casualties	H.H.
BOVES	3		The Battalion moved at 4 p.m. by march, into billets at AUBIGNY near CORBIE. Advanced Transport at BLANGY TRONVILLE, remainder at ST. ACHEUL near AMIENS. No casualties	H.H.
AUBIGNY	4		At 9-0 a.m. orders received Bn. to be ready to move at ½ hours notice. At 10-0 a.m. order came to move, and Battalion moved, 270 strong, to high ground N.E. of VILLERS-BRETONNEUX, under 43rd Bde. During the day, positions were dug and taken up in support of 9th Bn. Scottish Rifles, and 7th Bn. K.R.R.C. with the 6th Cav. Bde (42nd Inf Bde) about on our right. Some advance by the enemy on our left flank. After dark Coys dug a new reserve line of rifle pits, each to accommodate 4 men, almost due North from VILLERS-BRETONNEUX, and occupied it. Casualties:- 2nd Lieut J.W. PYMAN wounded, 2-O.Rs killed and 11-O.Rs wounded.	H.H.
	5		Very heavy shelling on whole area from 11-15 a.m. to 12-45 p.m. Battalion remained in position all day and night. Casualties 1-O.R wounded.	H.H.
	6		Battalion relieved in the reserve line at 5-0 a.m. by 5th Aus. Div, and marched to AUBIGNY and thence to bivouac just west of BLANGY TRONVILLE with transport. No casualties	H.H.
BLANGY TRONVILLE	7th		Battalion moved by march to billets at ST. ACHEUL near AMIENS. No casualties	H.H.
ST ACHEUL	8th		" rested in billets. Transport joined Bn Transport and moved to unknown destination. No casualties	H.H.
"	9th		Battalion rested in billets. No casualties	H.H.

War Diary
or
Intelligence Summary.

M.S. Army Form C.2118.

Place	Date Hour 1918	Summary of Events and Information	Remarks
ST ACHEUL	April 10th	The Battalion marched to SALEUX and there entrained for GAMACHES. On arrival marched to billets at AIGNEVILLE. Transport at EU. No casualties	H.H.
AIGNEVILLE	11	Marched to EU and entrained with transport to HESDIN. No casualties	H.H.
	12	Arrived at HESDIN at 3.0 a.m. and marched to billets at ERGNY. No casualties	H.H.
ERGNY	13	The Battalion rested in billets. Lecture by Co. to all officers on DISCIPLINE. (No casualties)	H.H.
BEAUMETZ LEZ AIRE	14.	Battn. marched in noon via VERCHOCQ to billets at BEAUMETZ-LEZ-AIRE. Casualties nil.	H.P.
MOLINGHEM	15	Battn. marched 9.0 a.m. via ST. HILAIRE to billets at MOLINGHEM. 13 miles. The remainder of 3 Bdes of 14th Divn today reorganized as one Bde (43rd) of 4 Battns. 11th Bn The King's Regt. joined and 218 OR from 9th R.B. & 2nd Gloucesters (10 offrs) reinforced (10 offrs) Bn. Baffes and the Battn is reorganised from today as an Infantry Battn. no Casualties	H.P.
	16.	Remained in billets. 2 offrs +100 OR working party in the afternoon on GHQ line of defence East of Lt HAZEBROUCK-LILLERS railway. Casualties nil	H.P.
	17	8 offrs and 400 OR at work on GHQ line. Composite draft 60. from RB & Gloucesters arrived	J.C.C.
	18.	Work as yesterday on GHQ line, consisting of strong points, break works, connected up by trench works. Draft of 36 O.R.	H.P.
	19.	Work as above. Instruction in L.G.	

Army Form C. 2118.

WAR DIARY
or
INTELLIGENCE SUMMARY.

(Erase heading not required.)

Place	Date	Hour	Summary of Events and Information	Remarks and references to Appendices
MOLINGHEM	August 1918 20th		200 OR working on GHQ line under 413 Bde; 200 OR ditto under CRE. Both Batts.	
-"-	21st		Work as above.	
-"-	22nd		Work & training as above. 3 offrs. 202 OR of 19th Portuguese Inf'y Regt. now organised	H.P.
-"-	23rd		Work as above. as Labour Company; attached to the Batt.n for work.	H.P.
-"-	24th		Work and training as above. 1st Portuguese Labour Company began work	
-"-	25th		Work and training as above.	
-"-	26th		Work & training continued as above.	
-"-	27th		The Batt's C.O., a Batt. Training Staff & 10 offrs & 52 O.Rs returned for training American troops, went by rail to ETAPLES from BERQUETTE, on a.m.tt. 13 offrs and 640 OR. The Training Staff & Transport intact remain at MOLINGHEM awaiting orders.	H.P.

[signature]

WAR DIARY

of

11th Bn The King's Batt. Training Staff

From April 27th 1918

To May 31 1918

(Volume I)
(Battalion Volume No 36).

WAR DIARY or INTELLIGENCE SUMMARY

Army Form C. 2118.

15th Bn. THE KING'S BATTN. TRAINING STAFF

Place	Date	Hour	Summary of Events and Information	Remarks and references to Appendices
MOLINGHEM	27	12 noon	Batt's Training Staff from 11th & 13th Jn. King's Regt. now disbanded remained in billets.	A.P.
LISBOURG	28		Moved by march via ST HILAIRE to billets at LISBOURG, now 43's Inf. Bde.	
SAINS LEZ PRESSIN	29		Continued the march, 6 SAINS LEZ FRESSIN, via RUISSEAUVILLE, where Bn Staff went into billets.	
"	30		Training commenced with Rates Training Staff courses of musketry. L.G. P.B.T. & Company work. Parade for uniformity of dress	A.P.
MAY	1		Stood by pending move, worked for this afternoon. Carried on Training.	A.P.
CLENLEU	2		Bn Tr'g Staff moved with full Bn Tpt via ROYON & HUMBERT to CLENLEU	A.P.
"	3		CLENLEU remained in billets. afternoon came in P.M.B.T. commenced.	A.P.
"	4		As above.	
"	5		As above. Regt Transport inspected by B.G.C. 43 Inf. Bde.	140
"	6		Continued Training as above.	A.P.
"	7		" " " " Tactical exercise carried out	A.P.
"	8		" " " " "	
"	9		" " " " Tactical exercise	A.P.
"	10		" " " " Bn fin Transport left Bath by 10 a.m. to report to C.V.C.Q	A.P.
"	13		" " " " Physical & Bayonet Training and SA drill with & without arms	A.P.
"	14		Training continued	A.P.
"	15		Training as above	A.P.
"	16		" " "	
"	17		" " "	

WAR DIARY
INTELLIGENCE SUMMARY

1/8" THE KINGS BATTN TRAINING STAFF

Places	Date MAY 1918	Hour	Summary of Events and Information	Remarks and references to Appendices
CLÉNLEU	19.		Commenced first Musketry Course at QUILEN RANGE (General Musketry Course)	HP.
"	20.		Continued Musketry. After 1st parade 7.0 a.m.	HP
"	21.		Musketry. Warning order to move to RoYoN area.	HP.
TORCY	22.		Battn moved at 5.30 pm via ST MICHEL - ROYON to billets at TORCY (9 miles)	
"	23.		Conference at Bde H.Q. on Training and Discipline at ye present time.	HP
"	24.		Training as before	
"	25.		" as before	
"	26.		Tactical exercise carried out in conjunction with Training	HP.
"	27.		Training as before.	
"	28.		do — ; 30ᵡ range.	HP.
"	29.		do — ;	
"	30.		do — ;	
"	31.		do —; received warning order to move tomorrow	

14.

11 Leopolds
Vol 9

9-4